ART DECO BOOKBINDINGS

◑

THE WORK OF
PIERRE LEGRAIN
AND
ROSE ADLER

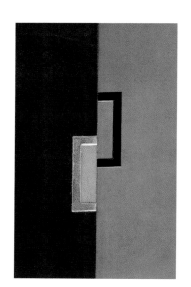

Yves Peyré and H. George Fletcher

ART DECO
BOOKBINDINGS

THE WORK OF
PIERRE LEGRAIN
AND
ROSE ADLER

Princeton Architectural Press, New York

IN ASSOCIATION WITH
The New York Public Library

Published on the occasion of the exhibition *The Art Deco Bookbindings of Pierre Legrain and Rose Adler*, jointly organized by the Bibliothèque littéraire Jacques Doucet and The New York Public Library

Presented at The New York Public Library Humanities and Social Sciences Library Sue and Edgar Wachenheim III Gallery February 27–June 12, 2004

Major support for the exhibition and this volume has been provided by The Florence Gould Foundation.

Support for The New York Public Library's Exhibitions Program has been provided by Pinewood Foundation and by Sue and Edgar Wachenheim III.

Published by
Princeton Architectural Press
37 East Seventh Street
New York, New York 10003

For a free catalog of books, call 1.800.722.6657.
Visit our website at www.papress.com.

Visit The New York Public Library's website at www.nypl.org.

Printed in Hong Kong
07 06 05 04 5 4 3 2 First edition

Translation of the French text by Lorna Kettaneh, revised and edited by Anne Skillion

For The New York Public Library
Manager of Publications: Karen Van Westering
Project Editing: Anne Skillion
Copyediting: Barbara Bergeron
Book Design: Suzanne Doig

For Princeton Architectural Press
Project Editing: Clare Jacobson
Cover Design: Deb Wood

Library of Congress Cataloging-in-Publication Data

Peyré, Yves.
    Art deco bookbindings : the work of Pierre Legrain and Rose Adler / Yves Peyré and H. George Fletcher.—1st ed.
        p.   cm.
    Includes bibliographical references and index.
    ISBN 1-56898-462-6 (alk. paper)
    1. Fine bindings—France—Paris—History—20th century. 2. Legrain, Pierre, 1889–1929. 3. Adler, Rose, 1890–1959.
4. Decoration and ornament—Art deco.
5. Bookbinding—France—Paris—History—20th century. 6. Doucet, Jacques, 1853–1929. 7. Bibliothèque littéraire Jacques Doucet. I. Fletcher, H. George. II. Title.

Z269.3.F55P49 2004
686.3'00944'3610904—dc22

2003023173

Frontispiece: Detail of binding by Rose Adler for Louis Aragon's *Le Paysan de Paris* (no. 36).

CONTENTS

FOREWORD

Paul LeClerc

THE EXTRAORDINARY richness of the collections of The Research Libraries of The New York Public Library notwithstanding, there are a few areas in which our holdings (even including our foundation legacies of the Astor and Lenox libraries) are insufficient to illuminate significant events in the history of the book. Certain areas in the art of French bookbindings—very imperfectly represented outside France—fall into this category. We have in recent years undertaken to alleviate this difficulty through cooperative ventures with collegial institutions in France. Thanks to our colleagues at the Bibliothèque nationale de France, we were able in late 2002 to present a once-in-a-lifetime installation of highlights from the era of the Renaissance. Our exhibition *French Renaissance Bookbindings for Henri II*, comprising a select group of bindings created in the mid-sixteenth century at or for the royal collections at Fontainebleau, showcased works of art that had never before left France.

The current enterprise—this volume, and the exhibition it complements— is the fruit of our cordial relationship with the Bibliothèque littéraire Jacques Doucet. A logical instance of cooperation for The New York Public Library, it enables us to demonstrate to an American audience a major moment in the history of the book. We are indebted to our friend and colleague Yves Peyré, distinguished poet and director of the Bibliothèque littéraire Jacques Doucet, for making it possible, and we are proud to be able to present the exhibition in the Library's Sue and Edgar Wachenheim III Gallery, which has been transformed into an appropriately elegant "treasure" chamber through the generosity of the Wachenheims.

But none of these activities would have been possible without the generous support of The Florence Gould Foundation, which has been crucial in our cooperative ventures with our French colleagues. Among the members of the board of the Foundation, Mary K. Young, knowledgeable bibliophile and learned researcher in the arts of the book, deserves particular recognition.

Paul LeClerc is President of The New York Public Library.

PIERRE LEGRAIN AND ROSE ADLER IN THE NEW YORK PUBLIC LIBRARY

H. George Fletcher

DURING THE PAST half-millennium in the West, French bookbinders have often led the way in refining and even revolutionizing the binder's art and craft. Most recently, in the earlier part of the twentieth century, especially from the 1920s to the 50s, French bookbinders fostered the designer-bookbinder movement that took such firm root in several other countries.

A major upheaval in the settled order of the bibliophile's world was the rise of Art Deco within the book arts, from the time of the First World War. The astonishing work of Pierre Legrain and Rose Adler exponentially propelled the binding into a new category as an artistic entity, while retaining its structural integrity. Legrain and Adler functioned as designers, leaving the bench work to skilled artisans at the top of their craft. Their patron, Jacques Doucet, fostered their best work and claimed nearly all of it for himself, so that the creations of both artists continue to be rarely encountered in the market. In other words, most of their work—or at least virtually all their freshest work—now survives in institutional collections in their native France. So, as is appropriate, the contribution of the Bibliothèque littéraire Jacques Doucet to the present joint venture constitutes by far the greatest part of this publication and the exhibition it records.

Historic bookbindings are widely represented in the collections of The New York Public Library, both within the Spencer Collection, the Library's principal repository of such work, and elsewhere; those in the Spencer Collection have been painstakingly gathered over the decades by two of its curators, the late Karl Küp and the incumbent, Robert Rainwater. It is worth noting that the Spencer Collection began as the bequest of William Augustus Spencer, an American boulevardier who had the misfortune to sail on the *Titanic*, and who himself collected finely bound art books in the Belle Epoque Paris in which he and his wife resided for many years.

Thus far, the Spencer Collection has become the custodian of six bindings by Pierre Legrain and four by Rose Adler, and one by each artist is featured here. There is also an immense album of Legrain's designs to which I shall return shortly, and it thus constitutes a seventh binding, with extraordinary doublures. While some of these have been acquired in recent years, the work of both artists is so infrequently offered that each purchase is a notable occurrence. (There is a published report that the Library commissioned Adler to create bindings for us. Alastair Duncan and Georges de Bartha's *Art Nouveau and Art Deco Bookbindings* states, "After Doucet's death in 1929, Adler began to concentrate on other major commissions, both for private book collectors and for libraries and institutions such as . . . the New York Public Library" [p. 186]. This report, unfortunately for us, is not true.)

One of the Legrain bindings in the Spencer Collection is on a copy of René Boylesve's *Souvenirs du jardin détruit* (Paris: J. Ferenczi et fils, 1924), inscribed by the author to Madame George Blumenthal. Another Legrain binding in the Spencer Collection, on Valéry's *La Jeune Parque* (Paris: Editions Emile-Paul frères, 1925), is inscribed by the author to Florence Blumenthal. These two bring us to the following somewhat confused issue.

A cohesive and choice collection of French literature in French bindings was donated to the Library in January 1937, and is named the George Blumenthal Collection after its donor. Florence Blumenthal, his wife, was a connoisseur of French literature and patron of a small number of French writers and designer-bookbinders in the years between the World Wars. The bindings she commissioned include work by Geneviève de Léotard

and Pierre Legrain. Ten Legrains are currently in the Blumenthal Collection, on a variety of essentially contemporary works. This group of survivors presents a statistical quandary. The catalogue raisonné *Pierre Legrain Relieur* (*PLR*) calls for twenty-one bindings commissioned by Mrs. Blumenthal, according to the account ledgers. But there are Legrain bindings in the Blumenthal Collection not recorded in *PLR*. And there are the Boylesve and Valéry presentation copies in the Spencer Collection, which are therefore the eleventh and twelfth Legrain bindings with a Blumenthal connection among our holdings. (The record is silent, but we assume that the respective curators of the Blumenthal and Spencer collections transferred these two books many years ago.) To compound the puzzle, one cohesive group of three bindings in the Blumenthal Collection is given a single inventory number in *PLR*, where one would have expected three separate entries. None of the Blumenthal commissions is described in detail in *PLR*. Even allowing for confusion and lack of precision, one could conclude that Florence Blumenthal commissioned perhaps twenty-three or twenty-four bindings from the Legrain atelier. Beyond this, even assuming for argument's sake the accuracy of the Legrain account ledgers, we have no information on the fate of those reported bindings beyond the twelve in the Library's keeping. One wonders if all commissions recorded in the account ledgers and then canonized in *PLR* were in fact executed.

Moreover, the Spencer Collection's copy of Georges Rouault's *Paysages légendaires* is recorded in *PLR* as a work for which Legrain designed a binding that was completed only after his death. It is the contention of the curators of the current exhibition, however, that it must be from among Legrain's very last bindings, and belongs to those completed at about the time of his death. There may well be further discrepancies, and the catalogue raisonné is, alas, not the final word on Legrain's achievement and legacy.

In 1970 the Spencer Collection acquired a royal-folio album of 96 original designs by Pierre Legrain, tipped onto the blank leaves of an elaborate polychrome mosaic goatskin binding that he designed. They date from across the dozen years of his brief career, and demonstrate that Legrain used the back of Doucet wallpaper that can otherwise be found as linings in certain of the bindings for his patron. Among the designs are two for Jacques Doucet's copies recorded in this present volume, the design for the rear doublure of the album itself, and the design for a volume in the Blumenthal Collection. Two variants for the design of an imposing quarto in the Spencer Collection, Alfred de Vigny's *Daphné* (Paris: chez F. L. Schmied, 1924), are also present.

This publication and the exhibition it accompanies capture very significant components of a signal moment in the history of the book and of literature in the twentieth century. We have before us not only extraordinary instances of the art of bookbinding, but also the works themselves, many of which constitute a unique legacy of French literary culture in the modern era.

Leonetto Capiello. Portrait of Jacques Doucet.
Ink and crayon, 1903.

JACQUES DOUCET AND THE ART OF BOOKBINDING

Yves Peyré

A BOOKBINDING is an ambiguous thing. It is physically attached to the book and thus relates to its meaning and typography; but it is also an image. Even more radically, it is a structure that rapidly becomes an object in its own right. Because of this, binding played a legitimate role in a period of artistic revolution, from 1870 to 1933, during which art expanded both its territory and its range of expression. A new freedom and inventiveness allowed bookbinding to move closer to the arts with which it was linked: poetry, typography, painting, sculpture, architecture, and furniture design. All these forms of creation would now advance in concert. The genius of the patron Jacques Doucet, as well as that of the designer-bookbinders Pierre Legrain and Rose Adler—in whose hands the modern book was born—lay in the fact that they did not isolate bookbinding from these brand new, completely reconceived forms of art, nor did they cling to old traditions or confine themselves to a limited professional circle. In short, they furthered the art of bookbinding—which in their hands became a major art in and of itself—and in their own work reached a pinnacle that invites very few comparisons.

More than any other art form, binding is closely allied to architecture, in that it relates to the world of objects in general, which, for lack of a better definition, we call the decorative arts. Architecture itself is as saturated with the spirit of poetry and painting as it is with that of industry. In successive thrusts aimed at forward-looking parts of Europe and North America, architecture brought about a profound break at the end of the nineteenth century and at the turn of the twentieth, and with it a change in the manner of perceiving and creating objects. Architecture had no desire to trail the other arts, nor would it tolerate being behind the times. In France, Mallarmé had reconceived poetry, both in terms of its meaning and its visibility, while Manet had shown the way to innovation in painting; Cézanne carried the break with the past even further, definitively creating the basis for a new way of perceiving the world. In light of such contributions, it would be sad to think that those enacting such formidable changes had continued to live in a bourgeois fashion, inhabiting conventional buildings and surrounding themselves with objects whose only claim to quality came from their antiquity. Against eclecticism, against historicism, against routine and mediocrity, architecture took it upon itself to react. A broad-based groundswell, albeit one with antecedents (the architects Joseph Paxton, Henri Labrouste, Gustave Eiffel, and Hector Horeau, for example), confronted conformity.

This revolution in the art of building and in the creation of objects found its most fertile breeding ground in the universal exhibitions (and similar events) that rapidly succeeded one another from 1851 on. There existed an incentive both to show off the new (in cities wanting to demonstrate their vitality), and to take risks (including architecturally) in the manner of presenting new ideas. Palaces and pavilions, nominally ephemeral, were erected. These transitory edifices served as excellent vehicles for advancing the audacious (the Crystal Palace and the Eiffel Tower are perfect examples). What strikes us initially is the force of the break with the canons of art based on antiquity. Art Nouveau, Art Deco, and Functionalism represented three distinct manners of creating this break with the past, and although they were often violently antagonistic, there is no doubt that they defined themselves by their distinctive responses to a common enemy—namely, eclecticism. The Austrian architect and designer Otto Wagner (1841–1918) can be viewed as the most convincing incarnation of this and can be considered the father of the three new tendencies. From the rounded suppleness of Art Nouveau to the geometric rectitude of both Art Deco and Functionalism (with or without ornament, so wide is the range), from the enthusiasm for manufactured goods to the exaltation of luxury, innovation pushed forward. Only the worldwide economic crisis of 1929 and the growing perils of the 1930s could slow the momentum that had followed the First World War. From 1890 to 1930, many participated in the new movement, each one seeming reasonably informed about similar efforts in other parts of the world. Although influence must not be underestimated, it is obvious that simultaneity was in fact paramount, which only underscores the supra-personal and supra-local qualities of this movement.

In fact, the entire Western world took part in the great change. The first indications came from Belgium (Victor

Horta and Henry Van de Velde made Brussels the capital of the new), although Scotland (Charles Rennie Mackintosh in Glasgow) and the United States (the Chicago School, with its emblematic architects Louis Sullivan and Frank Lloyd Wright) have some claim to being the first. Other countries figured prominently: France (Hector Guimard in Paris and Emile Gallé in Nancy), Austria (Otto Wagner and his disciples Joseph Maria Olbrich and Josef Hoffmann, as well as Adolf Loos, in Vienna), and Spain (Antoni Gaudí, alone and separate in his genius, in Barcelona). Italy and Finland rapidly joined the movement, which spread through Germany (Munich, Darmstadt, Berlin, Cologne, Weimar, Dessau) and to cities influenced by Vienna, either directly (Olbrich reigned in Darmstadt and Hoffmann gave Brussels its second wind) or indirectly (Budapest and Prague elaborated Vienna). Still other cities were clamoring to be heard: New York (where Art Deco triumphed more than in Chicago and where it was much preferred to pure, hard Functionalism; the Chrysler Building by William Van Alen serves as the most superb paradigm of this tendency) and, on the other side of the country, San Francisco (with its glorious Golden Gate Bridge). Shortly thereafter, Holland produced its unique approach. Everywhere, man's environment (his home) and his customary accoutrements (furniture and objects) were redefined.

At the heart of this abundant era, in Paris, a place particularly involved in these rapid changes, a second adventure, analogous to the first and largely dependent on it, was born. One man served as its pivot: Jacques Doucet (1853–1929). A brilliant couturier and one of the originators of haute couture, an important collector of Impressionist and eighteenth-century art, and a patron of artists, Doucet was no less inventive himself. In 1912, at the age of fifty-nine, he decided to change direction and put his renowned eighteenth-century art collection up for sale. In every way, he rethought his environment and readjusted his vision, definitively liberating his sensibility and his spirit. This about-face, in no way capricious, showed his strong desire to be in tune with the times in which he lived, to be a contemporary of a younger generation that reveled in a new art of living. Tired of the tried and true, he needed to feel the vibrations of the not yet accomplished, to experience the trembling of the new. Some time later, in 1921, he confided his intentions to the critic Félix Fénéon, saying that the break with the past had had to be both radical and global. In some respects, Doucet was only being faithful to himself; he did nothing but plant his feet firmly and joyfully on another shore, just as, at age twenty-one, he had wholeheartedly embraced the ideas of Impressionism, which remained, despite various changes of course, a constant in his life as a collector and as a couturier (his dress designs attest this).

Doucet fully understood that to restructure contemporary design would require commitment on several fronts. He would not abandon art in the form of painting and sculpture, nor writing in the form of sophisticated poetry and prose, nor furniture and objects, nor primitive art—painting, poetry, and the decorative arts were, for their inventiveness, prized by him equally. He even became involved in architecture with Paul Ruaud, principally in interior design.

He sought to acquire the best examples of modern art, while lending his wholehearted support to what would soon be called Art Deco. He knew that writing, the plastic arts, and decoration formed a single entity, and he felt a passion to seize, to stimulate, to radicalize, and to accelerate the spirit of his era, surely because he knew his vision was ahead of its time. From 1913 to 1929, Doucet determined to interpret in his own way the best of what surrounded him, and there he succeeded, in the most natural way possible, capturing all that was essential to express a completely new taste. In the field of interior design he solicited, both for his apartment on the avenue du Bois and for his studio on the rue Saint-James (both monuments to Art Deco), the collaboration of the best innovators in the fields of furniture and interior design—Eileen Gray, Paul Iribe,

Marcel Coard, René Lalique, Pierre Legrain, Paul Poiret himself, and many others such as Paul-Louis Mergier, René Moulaert, Joseph Hecht, Gustave Miklos, Rose Adler, Joseph Csaky, and Etienne Cournault.

From 1913, Doucet also dedicated himself to building a collection devoted to French literature; this was the beginning of his great library. And it was with the advice and counsel of Suarès, Apollinaire, Cendrars, Reverdy, Breton, Aragon, and Desnos that Doucet created a literary collection of a kind that he had scarcely dared to imagine, preserving memory through the media of the manuscript and the rare book (in all senses of the term), conferring for the first time a patent of nobility on correspondence. From the early innovators desirous of making a break with the past (Baudelaire, Rimbaud, Mallarmé, Verlaine) to the masters of the written word (Claudel, Valéry, Gide, as well as Jammes, Gourmont, Suarès), from the pillars of the modern spirit (Apollinaire, Cendrars, Reverdy) to the most recent writers (Breton, Tzara, Desnos, Leiris, Eluard, Crevel, Aragon), from Symbolism to Surrealism, including Cubism, Dadaism, and even the various forms of Classicism—all found a place in Doucet's fervent temple.

At the heart of this library, which soon became legendary (and which grew to become both quantitatively and qualitatively the best repository of modern French literature), it fell to the art of bookbinding

◤ **D'Ora. Portrait of Pierre Legrain, 1920.**

twenty-seven-year-old graphic designer named Pierre Legrain (1889–1929). Because of a heart ailment, Legrain had been discharged from volunteer service in the French Army, and wartime conditions made it difficult for him to find work.

Legrain had previously worked for Doucet, but the latter was unaware of this fact. Legrain had worked for several years in the shadow of Paul Iribe, one of Doucet's favorite decorators and a specialist in innovative furniture. Legrain had created models for Iribe and more than once inspired the great designer with his sense of draftsmanship and of a subtle simplicity so impressive that it seemed equivalent even to that of Mackintosh and Hoffmann (the wonderful desk by Iribe after Legrain's design, all in straight lines except for the ovals found in the decorative elements, and its rounded chair, both preserved in the Bibliothèque littéraire Jacques Doucet, serve as the best examples of Legrain's influence on Iribe). A genius had emerged, eager to demonstrate his talent, and well aware of Doucet's creative aspirations and his propensity for audacious breaks with the past.

Doucet—living in the moment, thinking about his library, and the books and original manuscripts that needed protection—blurted out something on the order of, "What if you made me some bookbindings?" Although he was impatient to work, Legrain was dumbfounded by Doucet's proposition. He knew nothing

to form a point of juncture between writing and architecture (in its largest sense, as the science of the object). During the First World War, when the library, already largely assembled, had passed through the difficult early period of its founding, Doucet encountered an obstacle. He wished to protect his manuscripts and rare books (some issued as unbound sheets, some in paper covers) and to go even beyond this. It made sense to give them bindings, but bindings that wouldn't be jarring; that is to say, bindings of a sort that did not yet exist. Doucet waited. Then, in 1916, he received a visit from a young, unemployed artist, a talented about binding; he declared his incompetence. Doucet did not give up; he argued that the bindings suitable to his books did not exist, that the right bindings were yet to be invented, and that despite the large number of binders in Paris, there was none who was up to the task. He noted that the important thing was to have a sense of matter and form (a strength of Legrain's), adding, to reassure the unhappy young man, that his job would be to create the maquette and that an artisan would execute the work. (René Kieffer, Germaine Schroeder, Henri Noulhac, and Georges Canape were among the highly skilled artisans who would execute bindings based on Legrain's designs.)

In this short interview, Doucet converted Legrain to the art of bookbinding, and in doing so awakened the talents of one of the greatest binders of modern times (only Rose Adler would equal him). The extraordinary inventiveness that Legrain exhibited from the very beginning owed a great deal to his inexperience. Doucet gave him carte blanche, his guidance consisting of little more than meaningful silences, elliptical comments, and some ideas about artistic truth. For more than three years (1916–19), he worked for Doucet on a monthly salary, delving into his books and manuscripts in order to create a unity of ornament that echoed the superior coherence of the collection. Of the total of 1,236 bindings that have been officially attributed to Legrain, 378

⇘ **Four simple bindings by Pierre Legrain for works by Pierre Reverdy: three three-quarter bindings combining leather and paper (*Le Voleur de Talan*, 1917; *Poèmes en prose*, 1915, standard edition; *Poèmes en prose*, 1915, deluxe edition) and one binding in paper boards (*La Lucarne ovale*, 1916). These four bindings were conceived in 1918.**

were created for Doucet, 358 of them during those three years. Only an additional twenty were produced for Doucet later, fourteen of them in 1920, and six after the period of the exclusive commission. (For a long time it seemed impossible to date the first bindings by Legrain, but an attentive examination of the materials used, the decorative elements, and the particular styles now permits precise dating of each binding. It can be seen that a binding executed in 1917 does not at all resemble one created in 1919.) In terms of sheer numbers this is impressive enough, but it is even more extraordinary in terms of quality, as the bindings made for Doucet are particularly inventive. It is as if, through the dialogue between them, Legrain was driven to a new level of audacity.

Within a few short years, Legrain attempted everything: his work provided the ultimate rationale for the spare binding. He was willing to use his magnificent talent for the most modest protective bindings: his half-bindings; his wrapper/slipcases that repeat a motif over several texts, such as his work for Flaubert (see illustration at right); the beauty of the paper; the cut-out design on simple sheep leather; the silver pearls affixed by means of a fillet—all this evincing a deliberate humility that nonetheless mobilized his creative energy. He was often satisfied with the minimal: one thinks of the voluptuousness of the trifles that he created for Reverdy, either by means of hard-grained leather half-bindings—with crenellations or cloth margins—allied to the vellum or the hand-made paper, or by means of a humble board binding, such as appears, as if tran-scendent, on *La Lucarne ovale* (see illus-tration on facing page). The *frisson* that animates such works is the product of economy and inspiration. As a graphic designer, Legrain raised to a new level the importance of repudiating all insistent effects; is this not the lesson learned from the Asian concept of minimalism? And he vigorously brought out the nobility of pure materials (whether leather or paper).

The one invariable element of his work was the primacy of place he gave to

⌲ A half-binding (*Lettres à George Sand*, 1884) and a paper cover with wrapper and slipcase (*Trois contes*, 1877) by Pierre Legrain for works by Gustave Flaubert. These two bindings were conceived in 1917.

the title and the letters themselves, around which a new kind of space was articulated. With Legrain, the geometry of the design became fused with the title, either hori-zontally or vertically, the binding the dis-crete preamble to the intense and sacred act of reading and the perfect pendant to the gesture of writing.

In their working relationship, Legrain and Doucet followed a logical pattern in which routine and daring were systematically paired: orderly work on a sequential schedule obviated the risk of scattered attention, while the obligation to create variety arose from within the works being bound. Prestigious collections began to emerge as soon as Legrain created series with infinite variations of form and materials (he was to triumph in this respect with the work he did for Gourmont; see nos. 4–6). He constantly renewed his perspective and *modus operandi*, imagining several types of bindings for the same author, from the most modest to the most sumptuous, from those that were almost abstract to those that were resolutely decorative, but always keeping in mind this declaration: "Above all, let us not *over-embellish* the art of binding, which is likely to die from embellishment. Let us do away with the traditional dentelle borders, the old printer's fleurons, the complicated mosaics, and the prominent raised bands that divide the spine compartments. Instead, let us view the totality of our current aesthetic desires, taking our inspiration from this potent blossoming of new industries that is transforming life as well as art."

It is sometimes difficult to untangle Legrain's creative course with each binding because of his characteristic restraint, which was a first principle to him. In any case, he made his superior sensibility prevail, by decisiveness, by bold shapes, and by an always refined simplicity; spare on the surface, these coverings are aquiver with subtleties. One can, however, easily distinguish between the spare bindings (where paper takes the place of leather); the simpler bindings, whose mode of expression is in a simple, subtle nuance; the bindings that although simple are slightly more elaborate in their design; and finally the bindings in which the design asserts itself more strongly, while still staying attuned to the spirit of the text. Very often there is a carryover from one type of design to another, as if he were wary of creating boundaries that were too facile.

Legrain reserved his simplest bindings for avant-garde poetry: Reverdy and Cendrars were several times the beneficiaries. In 1917, the binding for Cendrars's *Les Pâques* (no. 1) provided an extreme case: a roundel of vellum edged in gilt centered on each black paper cover, representing terrestrial reality as well as geometric perfection, corresponding to two onlaid strips (front cover and spine) of black hard-grained leather, bearing the name of the author and the title. A similar example can be found in Cendrars's *Profond aujourd'hui* (also from 1917; no. 3), with its inventive structure and design, a superb encounter of painted paper with vellum, goatskin, and gold. (In 1920, Legrain created a slipcase for the manuscript of Jean Paulhan's *Le Guerrier appliqué* [no. 20] that returns to the interplay of goatskin, vellum, and touches of gold.) In 1918, on Gide's *Lettres à Angèle* (no. 12), Legrain incorporated a hint of luxury. Other bindings, like the one for Verlaine's *Les Poètes maudits* (bound in 1917; no. 10), exude a princely humility: a pattern or a black rectangle is extended by a silver square, repeated three times in place of spine bands, and heightens the purity of a brown-violet hard-grained leather. In 1917, for the corrected proofs of his *Cahiers d'André Walter* (no. 9), Gide received the homage of a stylized mirror (repeated on each cover, narrowing on the spine, and enclosing the title at the base) by means of a gilt line running through the dark-brown goatskin. For *Feuilles de route* (bound in 1917; no. 11), he is heralded with a cover bearing an elegant gilt title, above which is a gilt square repeated four times (mimicking the leaves of a book), exuding the voluptuousness of delicately polished brown calf.

As may by now be clear, Legrain did not adorn just any books with his delicate yet firm simplicity, because Doucet chose only the best for him: those modern authors whom Doucet considered supremely creative (and only contemporaries or those who seemed to be the wave of the future). Verlaine took pride of place with fifty-three bindings; there were thirty-seven for Suarès, thirty-five for Régnier, thirty-three for Gide, twenty-nine for Gourmont, twenty-six for Jammes, twenty-two for Claudel, fourteen for Apollinaire, and twelve for Maeterlinck, all of whom Doucet held in high esteem. These were the high points of Legrain's work, but he did not rest there. Doucet had other, more or less secret, preferences that Legrain understood should be equally honored. Cendrars and Reverdy, as well as Paul Dermée, were given particular attention on several occasions, as was Paulhan, for his *Le Guerrier appliqué*. Jean de Tinan

was not neglected, nor were Benda, Cocteau, Drieu La Rochelle, Huysmans, Max Jacob, Laforgue, Lautréamont, Morand, Rodenbach, Jules Romains, Salmon, Stendhal, Valéry, and Villiers de L'Isle-Adam. If one were to add a few other bindings, some quite simple, others more elaborate, made to cover texts by Barbey d'Aurevilly, Baudelaire, Flaubert, Gobineau, and Nerval, one would quickly realize that the bindings for works by all the great names destined to figure prominently in the history of modern French literature and in the catalogue of writers bound by Legrain were created for Doucet, who, unlike other sponsors, did not ask Legrain to bind older or conventional texts, or classics. Doucet's dream, both for his decorator-binder and for himself, was not to maintain the status quo but to forge a new path.

In 1919, Legrain created a tooled trademark that would subsequently embellish several bindings: an emblem depicting the book's owner as a cat, in a stylized rendition that uncannily resembled its master. The source was a mischievous allusion to a line from La Fontaine from his fable *Le Cocher, le chat et le souriceau*: "My son, said the mouse, this demure creature [ce doucet] is a cat." This emblem was to appear in the center of covers that bore no luxurious element other than the splendor of the goatskin; its last appearance was in 1923, on a background of aluminum over elephant-gray leather that

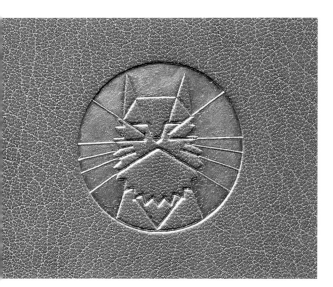

変 Legrain's famous trademark portraying the owner of the book—Jacques Doucet—as a cat. ("My son, said the mouse, this demure creature [ce doucet] is a cat," wrote La Fontaine.) From the binding for the manuscript of *Charmes* by Paul Valéry (no. 21).

clothed the manuscript of Valéry's *Charmes* (no. 21).

In reality, this sign apart, Legrain's only goal—both for modest bindings and more ambitious ones—was to interpret a title, to honor it, and to make its letters sing out. This he did in a remarkable manner for Gourmont, when he adorned the sumptuously colored goatskin with a most inventive frieze (part serpentine, part geometric), which wrapped around the spine and the two covers and came to rest at the foot of the binding. Nothing is more wonderful, perhaps, than the fertile

variation on a theme, created in 1917 solely for Gourmont on *Couleurs* (no. 4), *Divertissements* (no. 5), and *Les Chevaux de Diomède* (no. 6). One thinks of the somewhat equivocal *H* of the title and the well-considered motif for Apollinaire's *L'Hérésiarque et Cie* of 1918 (no. 13), of the concentric cover of Claudel's *Partage de midi* (no. 8), or of the mirror image of two other circles on Jean de Tinan's *L'Exemple de Ninon de l'Enclos amoureuse* (no. 7). Let us note also the vertical stripe (a black line between two gilt lines) duplicated nine times on the golden-tan goatskin chosen for Claudel's *Corona Benignitatis Anni Dei* (no. 2), whose only purpose seems to be to display even more beautifully, if possible, the central lozenge (enclosing the title), similar to the foliage of an abstract tree whose roots are composed of the author's name. And then there is the oriental stylization for Suarès's manuscript *Les Bourdons sont en fleur* (no. 18), where each gilt letter is encircled within a black roundel, all within an oscillating temple-like construction. Faithful to the mystery of the meaning that words can only suggest, Legrain hints at the infinity of the written word by creating a shorthand announcement through the title, which serves as the pivot of his construction, hovering between realized structure and an imponderable unfilled space that may actually be more real.

In 1918, four great manuscripts furnished him with the means to achieve this balance. First there was *La Ville* (no. 15), by Claudel, one of the authors who most inspired Legrain (only Gide, Gourmont, and Suarès could rival him). He dressed the manuscript in a simple yet beautiful olive-colored goatskin, framed by a gilt fillet similar to the one found inside. On the spine, sometimes in relief, sometimes not, the letters of the title appear in cascading style; at the bottom, more compactly, is the name of the author. The second great manuscript, *Tête d'or* (no. 16), again by Claudel, is covered in brown goatskin mounted on both covers against beige sharkskin; the title is relegated to the spine, where its letters are individually enclosed in gilt roundels (one of which is either imperfect or richer, displaying a thin addition for the accent). These same gilt roundels are found inside the covers on the linings of gold lamé fabric. Then, against this insurrection of empty space is counterpoised richness of construction, a completely different conception. Legrain utilized this latter method for the binding of Gide's sumptuous manuscript *L'Immoraliste* (no. 14), for which he proposed an alliance of citron and blue goatskin, the blue establishing its own specific structure within the abatement of a curve; he also used it for another moving manuscript, Apollinaire's *Le Poète assassiné* (no. 17), where he treated the title as if it represented an ascent from the depths, the letters rising in their lightness to become enshrined within the body of the

composition: black goatskin with a rectangle of red goatskin set in a border of gold. The title serves as both the frontispiece and the housing, Legrain thus glorifying Art Deco with the best contemporary typographic design.

In 1919, for the binding of Gide's *Le Voyage d'Urien* (no. 19), illustrated by Maurice Denis, Legrain elaborated a subtle ornamentation of interlacing figures whose aim was to better highlight the title and the name of the author (in this case, both were treated equally). More precisely, he did this for one of the two bindings with variations in color, not for the binding of the published work printed on Japon but rather for the binding of the volume without text, also on Japon, containing the final proofs of the engravings: black goatskin with red interlacings, gilt letters, and touches of cardinal-red (as well as the fillets that double over the interlacings). The curve of the exterior presents a delicate counterpoint to the straight lines of the interior of the covers.

All of this belonged to Legrain's first period, a time of prolific innovation in the service of one entity, Doucet's incomparable collection, which in 1919 and 1920 was already highly sophisticated both in its scope and in its realization. Legrain, however, was to come back for a second time to his brief life as a binder (scarcely thirteen years), in order to complete his work. In 1923, he created a binding for Paul Valéry's *Charmes* (no. 21), part of the series known as "*au chat*"; in 1924, he produced one as a complement to a wonderful collection devoted to André Suarès's writings. In 1927, he elaborated the most adventurous of his bindings, indicating a departure, a shift, in his work, which projected him firmly into the future. He created for Morand's *Les Amis nouveaux* (no. 22) a beautiful half-binding consisting of blue calf clad in perforated nickel-plated steel. The stainless steel forms a girdle around the calf, and the calf revealed in each perforation bears a gilt dot. To the connoisseur, this appeared to be an homage to one of Otto Wagner's architectural masterpieces, his Postal Savings Bank in Vienna, the steel rivets on the binding's inside cover reinforcing this impression, as do the three stippled fillets on the spine (enclosing the title and the author's name in a beautiful rectangle), and those on the interior of the covers. Here we have the most obviously "modern" binding.

In 1928, he produced his last bindings for Doucet, for the little magazine *Vers et prose*, for Paul Verlaine's *Chansons pour elle*, and for André Salmon's *Le Calumet* (no. 23), his ultimate contribution to Doucet. For the latter, Legrain once again used his favorite black goatskin, to which he added disks of green goatskin, reminding one of his predilection for concentric designs (previously used for Claudel's *Partage de midi* [no. 8]). The title leaps forth from the volute, tooled in thick aluminum. It also appears on the spine, as does the name of the author; in similar fashion, a thick aluminum fillet underlines the front and back covers, on the top as well as on the bottom, sometimes interrupting itself. On the interior one finds a mosaic variation of the same black and green goatskin, with the thick aluminum fillet on the top, interrupted in the middle, framing the green faille doublure with a band composed of thick, tightly spaced aluminum dots.

This binding for *Le Calumet* appears more classic than the one for *Les Amis nouveaux,* and it incorporates all of Legrain's experience from his earliest work to the point of his greatest success. All of Legrain is concentrated here: the soundness of his taste, his handling of rare materials, the intrusion of the new, and the trimmings reminiscent of the period of wartime scarcity, when he rummaged from the couture house in order to finish the interiors of his bindings. *Le Calumet* represented, as it turned out, a final homage to Jacques Doucet, the fervent advocate of books who had persuaded Legrain to become a binder. Pierre Legrain died of a heart attack in 1929, at the age of forty.

From the beginning, Legrain effected a profound shift in the art of bookbinding, saving it from relegation to the minor arts. He dreamed with a ruler and a compass; he gave the letter, interacting with the title, a central place; he invented a typographical rendering of immense precision. He played with form;

his geometric shapes were so delicate they seemed to flutter. In 1916, 1917 (his most fertile year), 1918, and 1919, Legrain brought to what would soon be named Art Deco an unexpected proof of the rightness of his approach (it seemed easier to rethink the forms of ordinary objects than to reveal a book through its cover). And Legrain was a necessary step on the road to Art Deco, certainly with his furniture and his creations, both past and future, as a decorator, but no less through his bindings. Thus the Art Deco bookbinding was born, but in reaction to what? Obviously to traditional bindings, which were too out of date, but equally to an earlier shake-up instigated by Henri Marius-Michel, who had been the first to try something out of the ordinary by covering his books with floral decoration influenced by the Art Nouveau movement. Marius-Michel, who like Legrain worked in the Val-de-Grace quarter of Paris, was no minor figure. He gave a new direction to his trade as well as to his artistic reputation by being the first to propose emancipation from the past. He is an essential link between past and present and his revolt is very affecting, but it is a minor one in comparison to Legrain's. (It is almost as if a bold reform had preceded a revolution, which would in turn upset the entire field of action and give action itself a new meaning.)

In his desire not to overuse decoration and in his passion for rare materials, Legrain allied luxury and simplicity, one of the hallmarks of Art Deco. Thus he joined Doucet, who had never completely subscribed to Art Nouveau, astonishing as this may seem (he was perhaps too partial to the rounded forms of the eighteenth century, and he certainly had an inclination toward Impressionism, although his dresses sometimes evoke Art Nouveau, even when they specifically refer to Impressionism). Doucet was also suspicious of Functionalism, which tended to mix the beautiful with the industrial. He definitely disliked ornament, as he felt it compromised form (in this he was closely allied to the modern movement of Vienna, Glasgow, Chicago, and Paris). He did, however, introduce the use of precious materials to enhance form and to give it a hidden throbbing ornamentation from within. (It was here that he embraced Art Deco and deviated from Functionalism. He was far from the tenets of the Bauhaus, as he preferred the refinement of handcrafted objects to mechanical precision. No matter what he may have said, the couturier broke through always.) Doucet, like Legrain, defended the principles of geometric purity, but in combination with the lyrical and, when necessary, the voluptuous. He prized art that breathed and trembled. He shared this with Legrain, and very soon Rose Adler too was to bring her inimitable touch to this work. Thanks to Doucet, Legrain, and Adler, Art Deco at its peak infused the world of books, released the floodgates, and bestowed solid substance on the ray of light that was Doucet's library. Along the way, bookbinding became a major art.

With Legrain, Doucet gave impetus to the modern binding. But to this fulfillment of his aspirations there was an equally inspired sequel. In 1923, Doucet and Legrain visited the Pavillon de Marsan where some of the students from the Ecole de l'Union Centrale des Arts Décoratifs were showing their bindings. Among the exhibitors, Doucet noticed a young blonde woman whose work captivated him. Rose Adler (1890–1959) had been hard at work for over a year and, with the help of her professors, had realized her first bindings, in which she attempted to equal the refined execution she found in the works of the great gilders, which she would always find dazzling. Doucet realized at once how he might take advantage of her superior gifts, recognizing the early signs of a talent that promised to expand and blossom.

Doucet was to regard this first encounter, under the approving eye of Legrain, as crucial, forever marking Adler as an exception to the flood of Legrain's unimpressive imitators. Mesmerized by her talent, he immediately ordered three bookbindings from her. The first was for Larbaud's *Beauté mon beau souci*, Doucet suggesting that the decoration for this book be identical to one she had created for a 1922 binding for Villiers de L'Isle-Adam's *Trois contes*, which had already been exhibited. It consisted of a superb geometry of lines alternating with an impression of tooled gold, receding on emerald-green goatskin from the spine, whose black base served as the titled centerpiece of its light structure. (This binding was acquired by the Bibliothèque littéraire Jacques Doucet only in 2002. Strangely enough, Doucet himself had not attempted to buy it, most likely because it had been previously acquired by another bibliophile.)

The second commission was for Toulet's *Les Contre-rimes*, on which a jade-green hard-grained leather with a very simple but constructed design was outlined by gilt fillets that flared out gracefully, coupled with an inlay of gray goatskin threaded with gold, ending at an angle. The third was for the sophisticated binding for Aragon's *Anicet*. Here, Adler's talent for formal innovation was at its height. In the center of the citron goatskin front cover and on the compartmented spine, she placed a mosaic design reminiscent of a stylized flower, mixing subtle grays, jade greens, and black, all set with gold. This was a splendid homage to Art Nouveau, but the inside of the binding revealed another message: the gold lamé doublure was separated from the citron goatskin by a jade-green and gray fillet, set with gold in the most beautiful Art Deco manner, accentuated by its refined geometry. The clash of desires expressed in this binding translated into an easy, integrated whole, demonstrating Adler's capacity to go beyond style to achieve a completely personal expression, but one that acknowledged its roots.

With these first bindings commissioned from Adler, something in Doucet caught fire. He seized with delight this extraordinary work, which went a long way toward meeting his expectations of Art Deco in its application to the book. He could see that this elegant, light-hearted, imaginative woman would be able to continue the momentum begun by Legrain. In fact, of all the talented students of the Ecole who were taught by the great gilders Adolphe Cuzin and Henri Noulhac, only Rose Adler would reach the level of a pioneer in the field by introducing something entirely new. The sense of the lyrical that marked her inventiveness allowed bookbinding to attain an undeniable historic stature. With her, modern binding was to reach its highest summit.

To fully appreciate Adler's significance and her precise contribution, it is important not to think of her as Legrain's pupil, or as the most talented of his disciples. In relation to Legrain, whom she admired and respected, Adler never assumed the posture of a follower. Nor was she merely a product of her times. She sought to translate a world of forms and impressions that already existed within herself. With regard to Legrain, she was an emulator, a rival, but also his equal, with her own personal talent. Adler's diffidence and her gratitude toward the pathfinder

⬊ **Al. Fasimi. Portrait of Rose Adler, 1932.**

Legrain led her, more than once, to downplay the evidence of any competition. Doucet, always clear-sighted, understood this, and it was among the reasons that he hired Adler and no one else.

Much like Legrain, who at a very young age had to overcome illness and other adversities, Adler—despite her flair and enthusiasm—was not spared the somber side of life. When her fiancé was killed in action during the First World War, something profound in her life was lost. No doubt it was fidelity to her first destiny—to live a life of writing and poetry with her great love—that pointed her toward bookbinding, even if it was in fact one of the best ways for her to express her multiple gifts. Building the thin protective cover of a book was, after all, not so different from what visionary architects and designers had been doing for some time, namely, rethinking man's habitat. Bookbinding, when submitted to this standard, decidedly attained the measure of a true art.

Adler quickly felt at home in Doucet's library, where she found fertile ground for her passionate imagination. From 1923 to 1929, she invested her talents in transforming something used merely for protection into a thing of beauty, a task that came naturally to her. (Like Legrain's designs, Adler's were executed by skilled artisan binders.) In 1924, a binding for Larbaud's *A. O. Barnabooth* was the vehicle for a sudden acceleration in her development. This splendid mosaic creation confirmed the design augured in the composition for *Anicet*, with an interior surface in no way inferior to the covers, taking the best from an approach already established by Legrain.

In 1925, Adler awoke completely to her inner voice, manifesting the two tendencies that coexisted within her: one part construction, captured by rhythm and fullness of movement, the other part clearing away any obvious frame, leaving room for a slight lyrical murmur of matter. Doucet encouraged her in this leap into the absolute by offering her the rarest editions of Mallarmé, Apollinaire, Reverdy, and Aragon. This is how the binding for *Calligrammes* (no. 25) on Japon ancien came into being: through a rigorous sense of architecture, confirmed by the affirmation of the triangle in which the suppleness

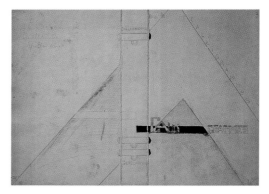

⬎ **Three states of the maquette for Rose Adler's binding for Guillaume Apollinaire's *Calligrammes* (no. 25).**

of the leather (ivory calf, beige goatskin, black calf) gently breathes, attenuating the rigor of the title and name of the author, with highlights of aluminum fillets, wherein the doublures do not repeat themselves (the first instance of the famous interior double motif), and creating a climate opposite to that evoked by the exterior of the binding; in this case, the black calf dominates the geometric inlays of beige goatskin. Everything conspired to make this binding a masterpiece, a feat of intense discernment.

At the same time, Adler conceived a protective portfolio for Mallarmé and Manet's *L'Après-midi d'un faune* (no. 26) in the deluxe edition on Japon (almost as if, on a book of this stature, no fixed cover could do it justice, a wise decision), translating an ellipse of a haunted city or of some stellar choreography next to an

the natural goatskin—that is to say, an inversion of the tones in the exterior binding—a double presence, each time associating two nuances of goatskin, black and natural, while that of the back cover reduces that presence to one.

Also in 1925, Adler proposed a fluidly accented binding, a superb variation for editions of intransigent texts that were important to Doucet, Reverdy's *Les Ardoises du toit* (no. 27) and Aragon's *Les Aventures de Télémaque* (no. 28). They

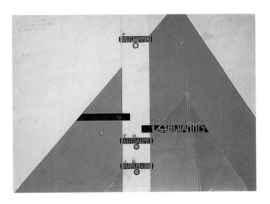
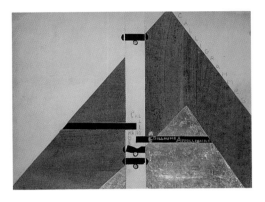

indescribable aquatic kingdom. The natural goatskin, the mosaic of pieces of black or jade-green goatskin and of lizard, the sparkling of tooled aluminum, all this profusion seems to sing the praises of the diverse elements, while the more sober doublures play off the same materials, the same tones, but tighten the thrust of the forms. It is the same refined manner as in *Calligrammes*: the doublure of the front cover presents, on a background of green goatskin inlaid on the periphery of

constituted twin bindings (like those of *Calligrammes* and *L'Après-midi d'un faune*, both executed by Adolphe Cuzin), which corresponded to, while opposing, each other: the beige hard-grained leather of the first, the black calf of the second; the same pattern of colored mosaic roundels on both; the very different spines (one mute for *Les Aventures de Télémaque* imitating, at the cost of a gold leaf broken by the simulation of two clasps of red calf, the spirit of the art of lacquer; the other very patterned, Japanese style, for *Les Ardoises du toit*, wherein the black and silver of the letters alternate on a hard-grained citron leather framed in silver, and introducing on the binding, one of the manifestos of Art Deco, a final homage, more touching than facetious, to Art Nouveau). One is astounded by the sensitivity of the doublures, the wrapper, and the slipcase modulating the motif; there is not one constitutive element to distinguish these two confetti bindings. Adler delivers a kind of lesson in voluptuousness and vibrating beauty, which she would always thereafter be fearful of failing to equal.

From then on she could attempt anything, and she did, in a most selective way, which characterized her style and forced her, in Mallarmé's phrase, to "sow in rarity" rather than in abundance. Like the year 1925, 1927 was unquestionably

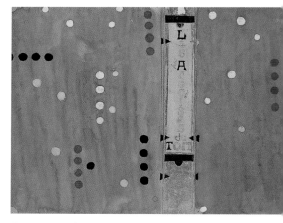

⬎ **A maquette for Rose Adler's binding for Pierre Reverdy's *Les Ardoises du toit* (no. 27).**

auspicious. In that year, Adler permitted herself new freedom. For a large and sumptuous yet very subtle binding, for Valéry's *Eupalinos, ou l'architecte* (no. 29), she reserved a white vellum from which arose sober inlays of black crocodile and light-tan goatskin as well as gilt tooling. The color palette and the association of materials ally this ample binding to a small series of vellum wrappers, lined with natural wood veneer, and accompanied by slipcases made of rare leathers (dark-gray snakeskin, green lizard, and the like), that she created for a few manuscript facsimiles (including Gide's *Si le grain ne meurt* [no. 30] and Morand's *Pluie vapeur et vitesse* [no. 31]). The manner of displaying the title, in single letters cascading down the spine, in an amalgamation of gilt impressions on the support (vellum) and letters tooled on the mosaic leather

⬎ **A maquette for Rose Adler's binding for Louis Aragon's *Les Aventures de Télémaque* (no. 28).**

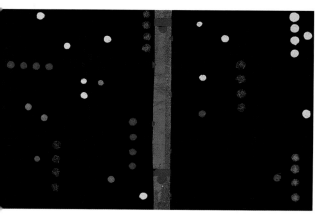

(goatskin, calf, or hard-grained leather), doubled the effect of proximity (the same idea was used, in all its splendor, for Leiris's *Simulacre* [no. 32]); the Galalith buttons, either black or ivory, reinforce the simple splendor that emanates in a spirit that Joseph Maria Olbrich, designer of the Viennese Secession Pavilion, would have recognized as his own. Because of the nature of its spine and its title, an equally modest design of 1929 (a simple binding made of vellum tinted jade-green, embellished with three progressively abating rings, like ripples in water), on Aragon's *Une Vague de rêves* (no. 38), was alluring because of its originality.

But there was more to come. In 1927, Adler elected, as she had already done with the wrapper covering *L'Après-midi d'un faune* (no. 26), to use beautiful scaly reptile skins (crocodile, snake, lizard), including them in almost all her compositions. This was particularly interesting for one who had elevated calf ("because of its feel," she once said) to its utmost dignity (as Legrain had done for goatskin, in spite of prominent graining and the boldness of the choice; to each his own leather). This is found on *Simulacre*, an immense binding (equivalent to Legrain's for *Tête d'or* [no. 16]) where the full black calf, whose matte aspect exudes elegance itself, is interrupted only by a section of red calf at the foot of the spine, and on the front cover by a half-oval of coral-pink crocodile, topped by an agate cabochon and

edged with a silver fillet. Herein magic was achieved by taking the risk of combining several superb formal devices from the second phase of Art Deco. Incidentally, in this binding Adler first adopted the practice of creating an inlay with a cabochon (lapis lazuli for Morand's *Poèmes* [no. 37], chrysoprase for Francis de Croisset's *Aux fêtes de Kapurthala* [no. 42]).

Again in 1927, Valéry's *La Soirée avec M. Teste* (no. 33), with its unconventional style, provided Adler with a final chance to implement an unsettling innovation. Here, the exterior and the interior of the binding are totally reversed. The front and back covers are clothed in gray snakeskin, the spine in red calf. In the middle of the spine and spreading onto the covers, one finds a simulated clasp (an architecture of black and red calf, of gray snakeskin, and of gilt tooling, the title and author's name divided between gold and silver). The doublure is of full red calf, simply imprinted with two black strokes and two more in gold, on the top as well as on the bottom, suggesting pincers; opposite, on the endleaf, one finds gray watered silk, calling to mind the tone of the snakeskin and prolonging the mirror-effect, the braided place-marker heightened by one light-colored coral pearl to complete the ensemble (there is an evocative echo of dissonance from another strictly contemporary binding, for Valéry's *Le Serpent*). We are left with an impression of great sensitivity, impeccable taste, self-effacement—a diffidence in homage to the glory of the work.

The year 1928 was to confirm Adler's gathering achievement and to witness the exploration of new paths that allowed her to assert her deepest preferences. With Morand's *Ouvert la nuit* (no. 34) and *Fermé la nuit* (no. 35), she created a diptych. Calf was used for both. Over the blackness of the first, Adler created a mosaic title, undulating over the front cover, embellished with different-sized spheres composed of concentric fillets of gold and aluminum. She placed one of those spheres on the back cover, and repeated another on the doublure of the same black calf. For the other volume she placed the mosaic title on the dark-gray calf, using the same capital letters, and created an aluminum curving fillet that prolongs the sinuous melody over the covers and spine. These two bindings represent the utmost in refinement, restraint in the use of luxury, and sensitivity in the use of form. They are nothing but accents and emphases. Immediately thereafter, Adler created a sturdier construction for Morand's *Poèmes* (no. 37). Again the black calf is heightened by the inlay on the front cover of a beige calf rectangle, topped by a blue cabochon fixed at the midpoint of the cover between the two lines of an aluminum arrow; on the spine, the square display of the aluminum title recaptures the look of the two preceding bindings for Morand.

At the same time, Adler created a binding for Aragon's *Le Paysan de Paris* (no. 36) in which she enhanced the subtlety of the colors of the calf, equally matching the black and green, carrying the link further through the simulation, slightly off center, of a double clasp, the gray calf set within a gilt fillet on the black side, the beige calf set within a black fillet on the green side, the title and author's name at the foot and the top of the spine (in very ornate gilt capital letters), and the doublure made of gilt-lacquered calf with a discreet echo of the exterior motif for the signature.

If Legrain can be said to represent the early phase of Art Deco, Adler incarnates the later phase. She introduced a new suppleness and vibration, and awakened a sensual dimension of look and touch. Although her constructions were carefully considered, they give the impression of spontaneity. Invention was the result of dazzling intuition. Adler shied away from all geometric constraint: a slight quiver plays over her surfaces, the recognition of the unexpected is everything. The title was not necessarily neglected, but it became only one of the elements of the decoration, never the whole entity, and it might even be relegated to the spine or disappear entirely.

The fascination with which we view her bindings emanates from their ability to capture the eye. This ability is based on a unique science of color and the use of consistently daring materials: Galalith cabochons, wood veneers, strings of pearls, plastic, and exotic leathers. Adler championed both the pure and the simulated, simultaneously letting the richness of materials flow freely, and then restraining them to narrower confines. A certain languor did not detract from the force of her momentum; a sure hand scattered evocative seeds, like that galaxy of nearly imperceptible gilt dots on the orange

⇘ **Al. Fasimi. The interior of Rose Adler's apartment on the rue Cardinet, 1935.**

full calf of Raymond Roussel's *La Poussière de soleils* (no. 39).

Adler produced 145 bindings for books and manuscripts, far fewer (less than half) than Legrain, and, of this number, only thirty-one can be classified as sumptuous, mixing leather with other materials. Her ardent imagination needed pauses. From its beginnings, her career was anything but linear. Her creations came in spurts of inventiveness, breaks in the rhythm, which despite reprises, continuities, or echoes transformed each of her productions into a surprise or a fantasy. Adler's talent was rooted in freedom and in a sometimes mischievous sense of humor, and she had a far less systematic concept of binding than did Legrain. In this regard, she was not drawn to creating series with variations as he had done. With only two exceptions (the covers for *Trois contes* by Villiers de L'Isle-Adam from 1922 and for *Beauté mon beau souci* by Larbaud from 1923), each of her large bindings is unique, even if similarities exist (as in the strewn roundels or confetti on *Les Ardoises du toit* by Reverdy [no. 27] and *Les Aventures de Télémaque* by Aragon [no. 28], or as on the wrappers that enclose Mallarmé's *L'Après-midi d'un faune* [no. 26] and Limbour's *Soleils bas*, which exhibit similar tones of leather). Sometimes looser relationships are suggested (for example, in the different bindings exhibiting the inlay of a cabochon in the center of the front cover: *Simulacre* by Leiris [no. 32], *Poèmes* by Morand [no. 37], and *Aux fêtes de Kapurthala* by Francis de Croisset [no. 42]).

Nonetheless, the diversified concepts of ensemble, repetition, and variation are always present in Adler's work and ideas. She reserved them for simpler bindings and more modest covers. One of her most admirable contributions, well suited to the spirit of Doucet's library, lay precisely in her inventive application of these: from her cases made of wood veneer, lined with velvet paper, fitted with joints of the same color, enhanced with a Chinese closure as well as a piece of copper for the title, to her slipcases of nacrolaque and wood veneer with a piece of mother-of-pearl for the title, or again to her flapped wrappers and her cases of vellum and wood veneer, tinted light gray with the tooled title heightened by a double fillet tooled in gilt, and finally to her use of displacement, the spaces and modulations owing their presence to the use of color and materials that moderate the sense of repetition.

Also unlike Legrain, Adler did not use variant decorations on her large bindings, certainly owing to the dissimilar meaning she and Legrain intended for the relation between the binding and the text that it protects. Legrain came to binding via interior design. He was an assembler of forms, whom Doucet rallied to the cause of binding. Adler, on the other hand, belonged to the art of the book from the very beginning; binding was her terrain. And she appreciated the book and its text far too much to create a binding that would be merely illustrative; as she fearlessly wrote in a manifesto: "The modern binder's modernity lies in this: he is in the service of the text. He must hear it and must make it heard. He is wedded to it, and exalts it. Nonetheless, he must not describe it, as any description would be a mere illustration. Imagination has its own spectrum of colors and forms, and it is solely by means of intuition that it releases the echoes that emanate from the text. Formerly, binding was deaf, ignorant of what a book contained. The mass of books touched by the beautiful stamped signature of the eighteenth century mainly exalted the great house to which they belonged." It mattered greatly to her that the covers, the spine, and the interior of each of her bindings be in complete harmony with the text. In this sense, she was less distant from her subject than Legrain, and she dreamt of creating in her bindings a preliminary experience, translated into colored forms and strokes, of the words to come.

Again unlike Legrain, Adler made a sharp distinction between her great bindings and those she undertook mainly for conservation, or to satisfy the library's need for classification. Also, she was never an exclusive employee of the library in the way that he had been for more than three years. Unlike him, she did not create consistent ensembles devoted to one author, as he had insisted on doing (even though she returned faithfully to some authors, like Valéry, Aragon, Larbaud, Giraudoux, and Morand, and even though she kept coming back to Villiers de L'Isle-Adam, she preferred to honor unique bursts of creativity emblematic of an author, such as Reverdy's *Les Ardoises du toit*, Apollinaire's *Calligrammes*, Roussel's *La Poussière de soleils*, and Leiris's *Simulacre*, thus embracing an anthologizing spirit more than Legrain's encyclopedic tendency). Adler's relationship to the library was thus that of a maverick, an independent artist who found in Jacques Doucet her most ardent supporter and client. (He was also a friend, in some ways a father, and, even if only in an idealized sense, her Prince Charming.) Although she was less involved in the daily activity of the library than Legrain had been, Adler ultimately became closer to it, never tiring of it, perpetually attracted to it as if drawn by a magnet. Her partial distance from it served only to fuel her interest in it.

But Adler soon faced a difficulty: how could she pursue such accomplished work without lowering her standards, and continue to innovate without abandoning her style? With the last bursts of the enchanted collaboration between her and Doucet, the year 1929 reaffirmed that everything remained possible, even awaited discovery. First there was that minimalist insistence on a light (powder-like) deposit of gilt dots, a galactic curve on the orange of the full calf of Roussel's *La Poussière de soleils* (no. 39), the title mimicked, the text evoked in the evanescence of a murmur, the inside an alliance of orange calf and black calf, broken by an orange cut-out of a hemisphere and

gilt fillet serving to sustain it and to prolong the simple magic: one of the summits of an art.

On the other hand, as if to escape the attraction of the void, Adler proposed two eloquent designs, the first for Villiers de L'Isle-Adam's *Trois contes cruels* (no. 40), the other for Colette's *L'Envers du Music-Hall* (no. 41). The first is one of Adler's most famous bindings. From the matte quality of the black calf, a beige cylinder imaginatively detaches itself, turning around a thin purple line, from which a chain of gold roundels is repeated, this time strewn across the back cover; the aluminum title (except for two gilt letters and two in purple calf) follows the line and falls, slipping down on the adjective *cruels*. The interior simply picks up the clash of colors, beige being dominant, black and purple used only for the signature.

The binding for Colette evokes dance as conceived in the large Parisian cabarets, a style much used since Toulouse-Lautrec: it depicts an interplay of mobile constructions where the kicking limbs of the dancers intersect. *L'Envers du Music-Hall* appears on ivory-colored full calf, inlaid with royal-blue, black, beige, and red, with tooled aluminum and gold, in a complex but geometrically simple mosaic intended to express the curve of a woman's leg. The doublure reveals the inlay of a royal-blue calf rectangle on the ivory turn-in, and in the center, the play of the owner's initials

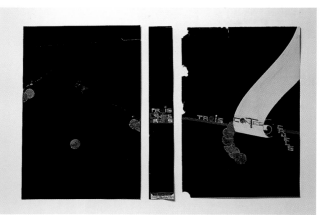

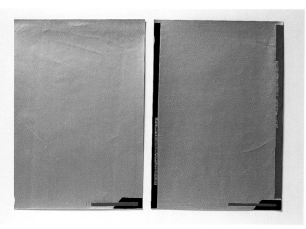

⬎ **Maquettes for the exterior (top) and interior (bottom) of Rose Adler's binding for *Trois contes cruels* by Villiers de L'Isle-Adam (no. 40).**

beautifully intertwined: J.D. revealed, or perhaps a presentiment of his death later that year.

The meeting between Rose Adler and Jacques Doucet was an essential one for him, as it prolonged, as if with a final burst of fire, his lifelong striving toward

creativity. A most felicitous complicity developed between a seventy-year-old man and a thirty-three-year-old woman, each pushing the other to achieve the best. Adler soon became Doucet's enlightened confidante and his trusted counselor. When Adler sometimes became fearful of implementing her most intrepid inventions, Doucet knew how to reassure her and validate her ideas: "My child, you remain perfectly classical," he would say. Some have suggested that there was a romantic entanglement; if so, it was apparently one free of the weight of reality, an idyll that brightened the final days of a great man. Doucet became reanimated by his contact with her radical daring and her sincerity, which was the essence of kindness. And Adler in turn admired his surety of judgment, his foresight, his audacity, his absolute freedom, and found herself drawn to this elderly man with such a youthful spirit. His library became her chosen territory and she loved working in it. Doucet gave her the opportunity to articulate, along with Legrain and himself, the direction of a modern impulse, through the very particular vehicle of bookbinding, so suited to form a bridge between the object and the book.

In 1929, at the end of a particularly gloomy October, three months after Legrain's death, Jacques Doucet's passing brought an epoch to a close. At the precise moment that Wall Street collapsed, heralding the end of an era, two major figures disappeared.

Adler was in deep mourning, having almost simultaneously lost her two partners in the far-reaching and remarkable adventure whose goal had been to elevate binding to a full-fledged art. Her distress, though, stemmed from the brutal loss of two friends, from the human dimension more than the creative one.

After Doucet's death, Adler remained involved in the activities of the library; she continued to contribute her own work, unfailing support, and advice to a place decisive for the book and for writing, one that from the beginning had charmed her, as if she had been introduced to it with the wave of a magic wand. In 1930 and 1931, prompted by duty to memory, by fidelity, and by her desire to maintain a life of innovation, Adler proposed, with the help of Lecarpentier as gilder (he had executed her precise and demanding designs since 1927), a last round of work in the spirit of Doucet, which endured within her. She created three bindings, all masterpieces, all quivering as if unburdened by materiality, spurning the ease and the eloquence of decoration (such is the effect of mourning), passionate only to express an allusion, aiming for the height of daring expressed with reserve, the dominant trait of Jacques Doucet's personality. Twice she created a full citron calf binding, for Francis de Croisset's *Aux fêtes de Kapurthala* (no. 42) and for Giraudoux's *Suzanne et le Pacifique* (no. 43). For the first she invented a slender gold arrow springing from a black base, growing at the center of a green cabochon topped with black fading rectangles, a pure and hallowed construction enclosing not only the book but also letters to Doucet from Henri-Pierre Roché and from a young maharajah who had admired Doucet. Doucet never read them; they arrived when he was dying. For the second book she created the sinuosity of a curve evolving into a spiral, and integrating within itself the design of the title. In 1931, for Louÿs's *Maddalou* (no. 45), Adler used jade-green calf and played with the letters of the title, in a style all her own; but the flat mirror images—empty space and fullness in equal parts—also served as a tribute to Legrain, and the sumptuous tuck of the doublure was undoubtedly an allusion to Doucet. These final bindings were both delicate and strong, insistent and evasive. A sense of reverie and depth prevailed, as well as her penchant for the play of vibration and transparency. This was the culmination of her and Legrain's quest. Years of greatness came to an end in 1931.

Twice Doucet had given binding its opportunity, and twice it had seized it. He converted Legrain and discovered Adler. The splendor of his collection reinforced his visionary perspicacity. Legrain and Adler were challenged by the distinguished quality of the works that Doucet put in their hands. It is noteworthy that they were afforded almost complete latitude, as Jacques Doucet advocated only freedom as the basis for creation. He intervened rarely; he gave advice sparingly, but his silences were eloquent and his sibylline words carried great weight; his influence was thus considerable.

This influence becomes evident when one looks at the work Legrain and Adler produced when they no longer worked for Doucet, from 1921, for the former, and from 1932 for the latter. Both experienced a certain falling off, seeming less in touch with the sacred and primordial restraint associated with Doucet. Legrain attempted more insistent ornament and at times flirted with excess. He no longer had the assured taste he had exhibited between 1916 and 1920, and which he quickly recaptured whenever he composed a binding for Doucet. Adler, too, was to become attracted to ornamentation. It would take the friendship of and a magnificent collaboration with the publisher Pierre-André Benoît (better known as PAB), as well as the affection of René Char and Paul Eluard, to revive the magic of her early years. Let us not, however, be too harsh. Legrain and Adler were in a class of their own, and not one of their contemporaries could even stand in the shadow of these two masters. This includes recognized figures (Paul Bonet, Georges Cretté, Germaine de Coster, and Henri Creuzevault), as well as long-neglected innovators (Louise-Denise Germain, Geneviève de Léotard, Marot-Rodde, Lucienne Thalheimer, the latter known especially

for her work with the Surrealist poets, starting with Breton).

Legrain and Adler were equals in their uniqueness. They invented an art, but with Doucet as a stimulus, and it bears repeating that Doucet chose only them (and also involved them in his other project, conceived at the end of his life, outside the library—his studio, where all the arts were to come together in an unforgettable personal temple of style). No one, at any point in the century, dared even to imagine rivaling the two of them; they reached a pinnacle of expression at a particular moment in time, with a fervor so intense that it could not continue indefinitely.

They would often shift the stakes. After 1920, Legrain created mostly furniture; he was above all an interior designer (his tributes taking the form of allusions to Africa, Asia, and geometric designs). After 1931, Adler too designed furniture, amused herself brilliantly with plastic fans and photographs, and created exquisite seashell tableaux that she framed with her usual excellent taste. But both artists remained faithful to the book, something they both loved, to the point that Legrain once seriously thought of designing a new typographical font. Hence binding was able to benefit, here and there, from this infatuation, through the art of surprise and excitement offering up a brief yet persistent perfume of the words it enveloped.

Legrain and Adler were only one year apart in age, yet one gets the sense that they came out of two succeeding generations. Legrain began his career very young and died prematurely, while Adler appeared on the scene only after Legrain had already realized a body of work, and after she had been detoured by a dreaminess that she saw as a fundamental element of her inspiration. Despite Legrain's elegance and his thirst for invention, his bindings remained faithful to a certain hymn to structure, typical of the first period of Art Deco. He remained instinctively at war with Functionalism (his personal taste, his entente with Doucet, the shortages created by the war—everything pushed him toward the strict economy of means that was his trademark). Having begun later, Adler benefited from the repercussions of the first wave of innovation. She had less to fight against and brought to the art a certain tenderness and languor.

Legrain and Adler represented two moments in time and two sensibilities. Their luck lay in the fact that their lives intersected with Doucet's and that they shared with him a period in history when everything—from the image to the art of living—was being completely rethought. Appearances changed (art, houses, furniture, objects, clothes); reality shuddered and reinvented itself. Doucet made a decision, and in response Legrain and Adler assured to bookbinding a place of honor amid the proliferation of undisputed arts (cinema and photography were to join this classic list). History was made, it accelerated, bookbinding entered the stream like a refined wave. Bookbinding asserted its prominence and, like a quiet necessity, let shimmer its prelude to the pleasure of reading.

Blaise Cendrars. *Les Pâques*. Paris: Les Hommes nouveaux, 1912. 16 pages. With a preliminary line drawing, in red, by the author. Autograph presentation inscription from Blaise Cendrars to Isabelle Bender. Autograph letters from Blaise Cendrars and Isabelle Bender to Jacques Doucet, tipped in. Design: Pierre Legrain, 1917.

Although this is one of Legrain's most modest bindings, he devoted to it an attention no less keen for its care not to distract from his taste for innovation. The interplay of simplicity and sophistication is inspired.

⤳ 2 ⤶

**Paul Claudel. *Corona Benignitatis Anni Dei*.
Paris: Editions de la Nouvelle Revue Française,
1915. 248 pages. Copy number 47 of 75, with
the text reimposed for printing on pur fil Voiron.
Design: Pierre Legrain, 1917.**

Here Legrain magnifies the verticality of the binding with a band duplicated nine times, broadening
into a lozenge for the title on the spine and into a
rectangle at the bottom for the author's name—an
allusion to a tree reduced to its own abstraction.

Blaise Cendrars. *Profond aujourd'hui*. Illustrated by Angel Zarraga. Paris: A la belle Edition, 1917. 48 pages. Copy number 1 of 5 on Chine, the gatherings variously folded; with a suite of five drawings (without colored highlights) and one original finished drawing. Design: Pierre Legrain, 1917.

This binding represents a major achievement: it is unquestionably the most ambitious of Legrain's simple bindings. The title, at the center of a carefully conceived architecture, is resonant, and the marriage of materials is magnificent.

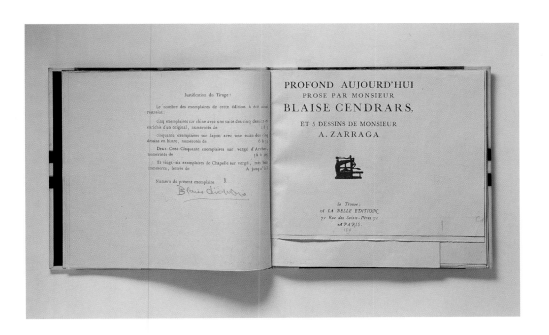

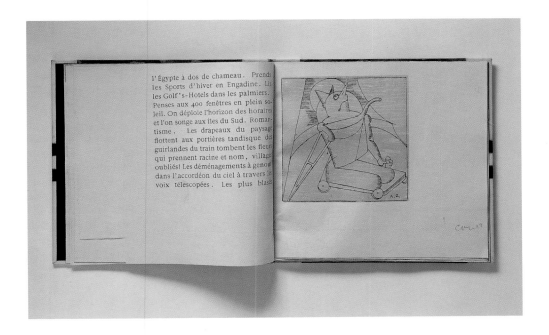

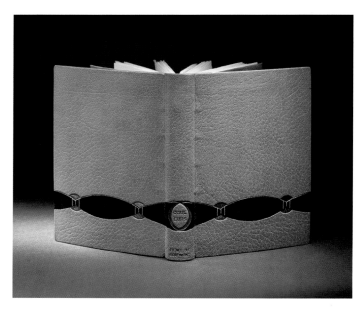

4

Remy de Gourmont. *Couleurs* [contes nouveaux suivis de *Choses anciennes*]. Paris: Mercure de France, 1908. 248 pages. Copy number 4 of 15 on Hollande. Design: Pierre Legrain, 1917.

Despite its apparent simplicity, this orange goatskin binding is more complex than the others in the series for Gourmont. Here, the frieze, while still restrained, is more figurative.

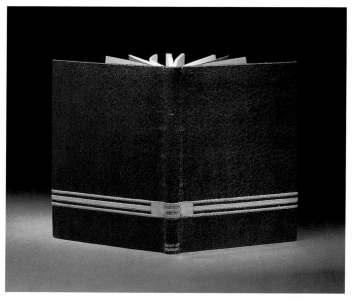

5

Remy de Gourmont. *Divertissements.* Paris: Georges Crès, 1912. 180 pages. Design: Pierre Legrain, 1917.

Voluptuously austere, this binding created for Gourmont suggests, through its geometric alliance of black and beige, the wish for the decoration to be secondary to the text that the reader is about to discover.

6

**Remy de Gourmont. *Les Chevaux de Diomède.*
Paris: Mercure de France, 1897. 256 pages.
Copy number 2 of 3 on Japon impérial. Design:
Pierre Legrain, 1917.**

By this flamboyant and serpentine, but simple,
binding, Legrain creates for Gourmont the motif of
the frieze, making the color and the goatskin sing.

⩗ 7 ⩘

Jean de Tinan. *L'Exemple de Ninon de L'Enclos amoureuse*. Paris: Mercure de France, 1898. 216 pages. Copy A of copies lettered A–Z, on Chine. Design: Pierre Legrain, 1917.

Down to the superb design of the large simulated clasp used to anchor the title, this binding combines a strong design with a certain roughness, a near-amateurishness, still possible at this early stage of Legrain's development.

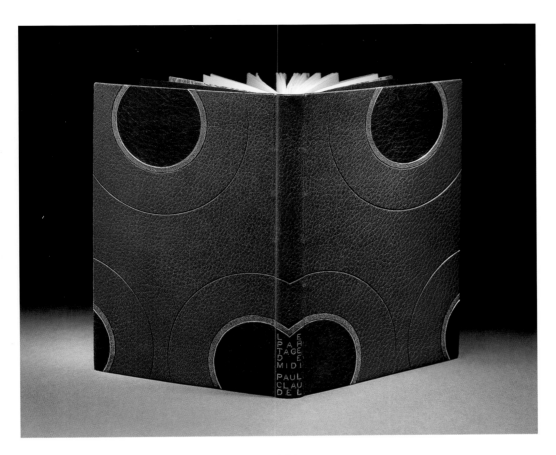

⤲ 8 ⤳

Paul Claudel. *Partage de midi*. Paris: Bibliothèque de l'Occident, 1906. 156 pages. Copy hors commerce. Design: Pierre Legrain, 1917.

An inspired concentric wrapping, evoking stellar immensity, this binding gathers the gold letters of the title and the first and last names of the author as if from the heart of a corolla opening out at the bottom of the spine; the entire binding radiates from this point. Trembling perfection.

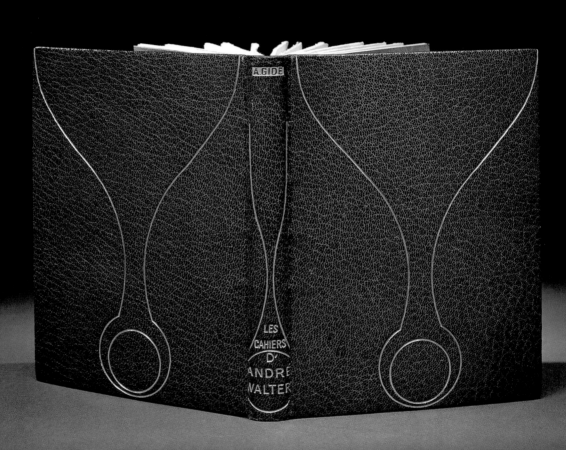

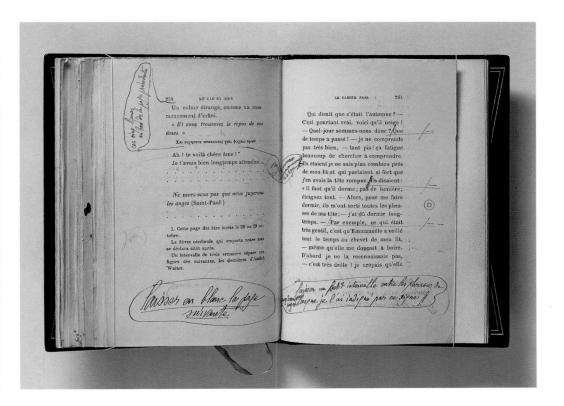

9

André Gide. *Les Cahiers d'André Walter.*
**Corrected proofs for the published edition of
1891. Paris: Librairie de l'Art indépendant. 256
pages. Design: Pierre Legrain, 1917.**

This small binding is a rare instance of resolutely
figurative although stylized work by Legrain.
The artfully repeated hand-mirror becomes pure
emblem on the spine.

The Bindings of Pierre Legrain ◗ 49

≥ 10 ≤

Paul Verlaine. *Les Poètes maudits*. Paris: Léon Vanier, 1884. 58 pages. Design: Pierre Legrain, 1918.

An unassuming tribute to Verlaine, the perfect musician of words. Here Legrain makes the nuanced tones of the leather vibrate, adding, only as highlight, a strong, thrice-repeated Art Deco motif: a rectangular strip of black goatskin extended by a silver square. Legrain repeated this structure on numerous bindings for Verlaine.

André Gide. *Feuilles de route, 1895–1896*. Brussels: Imprimerie N. Vandersypen, 1899. 76 pages. Autograph presentation inscription from André Gide to Henry D. Davray. Design: Pierre Legrain, 1917.

This binding, one of Legrain's smallest, looks like a manifesto of purity. The markedly geometrical décor, while seeming to represent a packet of pages, actually serves no purpose beyond extending the span of the title.

André Gide. *Lettres à Angèle, 1898–1899*. Paris: Mercure de France, 1900. 170 pages. Printed on Hollande. Autograph presentation inscription from André Gide to Louis Dumur. Design: Pierre Legrain, 1918.

The combination of bold construction and mixed materials makes this cover both simple and sophisticated, luxurious in its restraint.

≥ 13 ≤

Guillaume Apollinaire. *L'Hérésiarque et Cie*. Paris: P.-V. Stock, 1910. 288 pages. Copy number 8 of 21 on Hollande. Design: Pierre Legrain, 1918.

As the first letter of the title, the H is a fitting motif. Legrain extends the line, so marvelously light, from one edge of the binding to the other and even onto the turn-in, framing the doublure and traversing the bright pink goatskin, a color so appropriate to the spirit of Apollinaire. Never has a binder become so nearly a typographer, one of Legrain's enduring dreams.

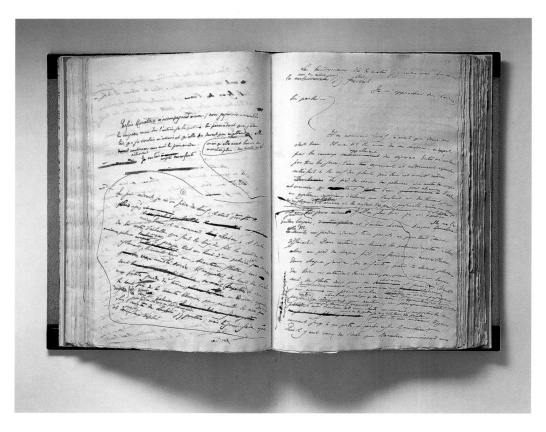

André Gide. *L'Immoraliste*. Manuscript.
225 leaves. Design: Pierre Legrain, 1918.

For this large binding on a manuscript of mythical stature, Legrain reduced the decoration to the title alone, modulated at the top and bottom with a dark wave that brings out the light in the citron goatskin. Inside, the effect is reversed: night dominates, and only a hint of daylight remains.

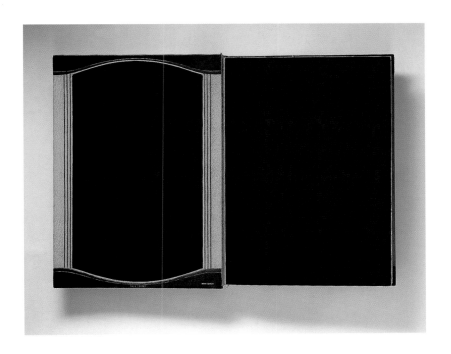

↘ 15 ↙
**Paul Claudel. *La Ville.*
Manuscript. 131 leaves.
Design: Pierre Legrain, 1918.**

For Claudel, who had always
been an inspiration to him,
Legrain returned to a beautiful
format with the plan for this
motif. Note the admirable play
of the simple goatskin musically
bordered by a full gilt tool, subtly broken at the joint. The title
and author's name emerge
from the spine like a caress
applied to the leather.

⤜ 16 ⤛
**Paul Claudel. *Tête d'or.*
Manuscript in two hands, a
copyist's and the author's.
280 leaves. Design: Pierre
Legrain, 1918.**

This is one of the most
beautiful of all Legrain's
bindings. Claudel's strange
manuscript, in which the
author's hand sometimes
alternates with that of an
anonymous copyist, is
covered in goatskin, which
acts primarily as a frame for
a panel of beige sharkskin.
From the density of the
materials to the pairing of
the accents of color, all the
elements bounce off the gilt
roundels on the spine and
the interior. This binding
seems to have no limits.

⤸ 17 ⤷

Guillaume Apollinaire. *Le Poète assassiné*. Manuscript. 153 leaves. Design: Pierre Legrain, 1918.

This imposing binding functions both as the frontispiece and the housing for another legendary manuscript. Legrain strives to lighten the heaviness through geometric composition, striking colors, purity of mass, and the title, which seems to emerge from the depths (and with *poëte* spelled in the manner dear to Mallarmé). Here, Legrain has mastered the spare sumptuousness of early Art Deco.

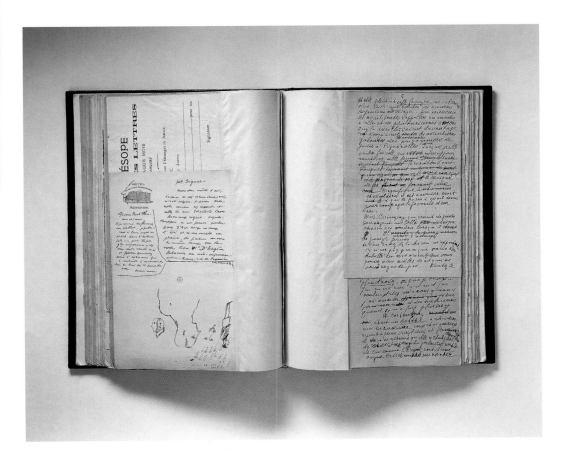

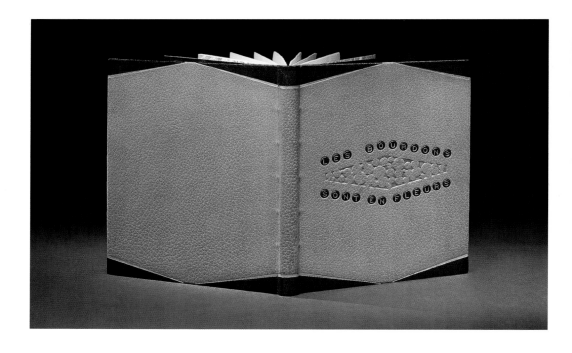

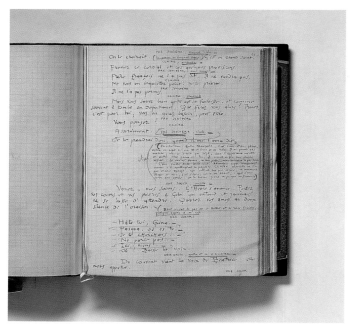

↘ 18 ↙

André Suarès. *Les Bourdons sont en fleurs*. Manuscript. 48 leaves. Design: Pierre Legrain, 1918.

On this binding, Legrain uses an astonishing oriental stylization to magnify the whisper of the title and the oscillation of the irregular shape, suggesting the roof of a temple. Legrain seems to be subtly subscribing to the sacred element summoned by Suarès's manuscript.

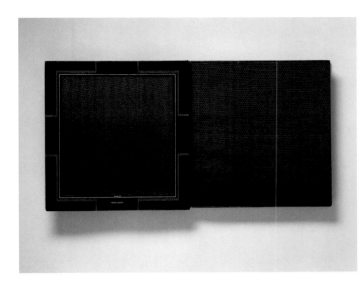

19

**André Gide. *Le Voyage d'Urien*.
Illustrated by Maurice Denis.
Paris: Librairie de l'Art
indépendant, 1893. 102
pages. A suite of lithographs
by Maurice Denis, proof before
letters, without the text.
Printed on Japon. Design:
Pierre Legrain, 1919.**

On the black background, red
interlacing encloses the title
within four gold corners in such
a way that the title appears
to be escaping. In this case,
Legrain astutely blends efface-
ment with firmness for Gide, with
whom he always felt a kinship.

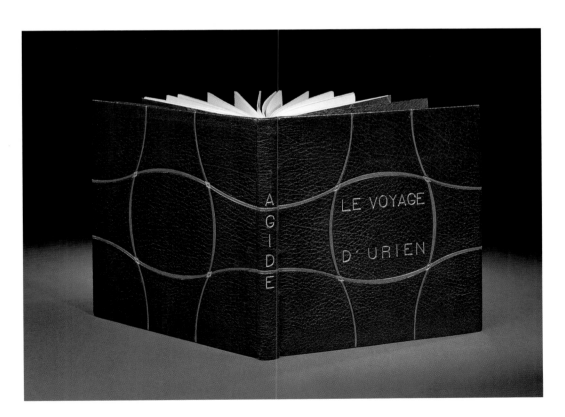

⇘ 20 ⇙

Jean Paulhan. *Le Guerrier appliqué*. Manuscript. 247 leaves. Design: Pierre Legrain, 1920.

The wrapper and slipcase combination that protects this manuscript by Paulhan is both delicate and strong, simple and refined. It whispers its essentials, adding geometrical elements as grace notes.

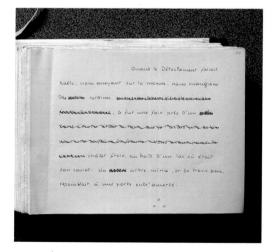

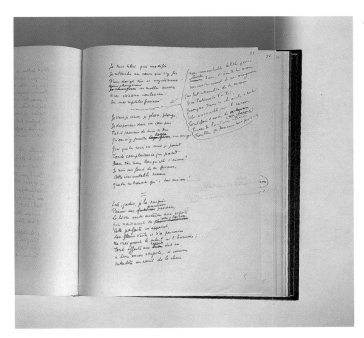

**Paul Valéry. *Charmes.*
Manuscript. 69 leaves.
Design: Pierre Legrain, 1923.**

Charmes, in manuscript, is the only text by Valéry for which Doucet specifically commissioned a binding from Legrain. It bears the trademark emblem portraying the owner as a cat, Legrain's deft visual pun ("My son, said the mouse, this demure creature [ce doucet] is a cat," wrote La Fontaine).

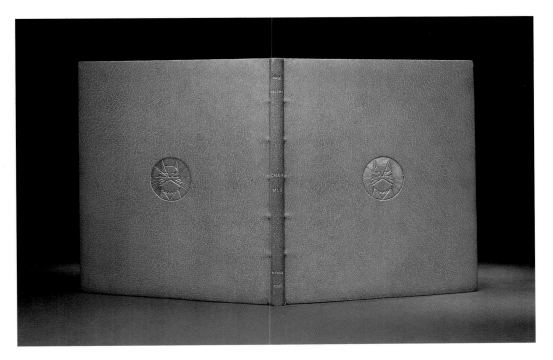

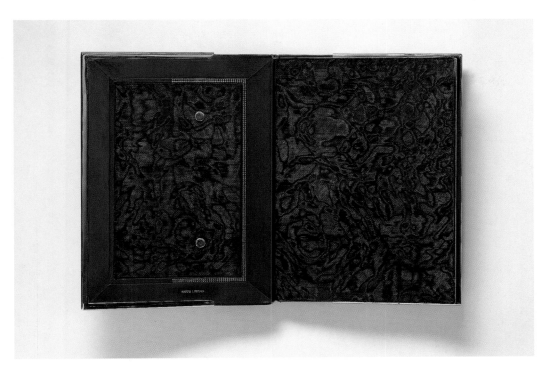

≥ 22 ≤

Paul Morand. *Les Amis nouveaux*. Illustrated by Jean Hugo. Paris: Au Sans Pareil, 1924. 40 pages. Copy number 21 of 30 on Japon impérial; with a suite of nine drypoints with watercolor. Design: Pierre Legrain, 1927.

One of the greatest modern bindings and indisputably the most emblematic of the new modernity, this composition, combining calf and nickel, is reminiscent of the architect Otto Wagner's great Postal Savings Bank in Vienna. The key element is the gold dots found in the center of each perforation in the nickel, as well as on the spine and the doublure. Through this binding, Legrain audaciously expresses the spirit of the Viennese Secession.

≥ 23 ≤

André Salmon. *Le Calumet*. Paris: Henri Falque, 1910. 132 pages. Copy number 6 of 20 on Hollande. Autograph presentation inscription from André Salmon to Jacques Doucet. Design: Pierre Legrain, 1928.

This binding, synthesizing Legrain's diverse styles, represents a revival of his great early period with Doucet. In this last binding conceived for Doucet, Legrain expressed the subtlety, economy of means, strength, and refinement that were always hallmarks of his work.

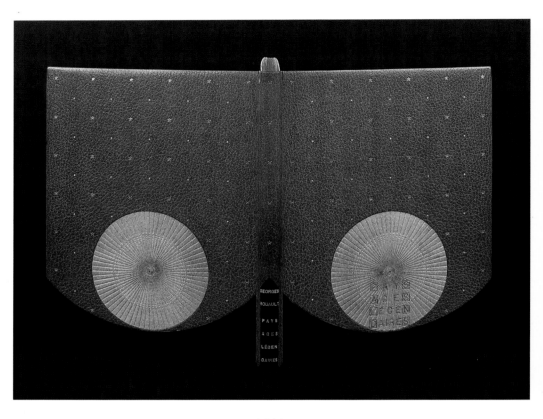

Georges Rouault. *Paysages légendaires*. Paris: Editions Porteret, 1929. Copy number 6 of 165; with a suite of eight original lithographs (two retouched), hand-colored by the author. Design: Pierre Legrain, 1929.

Legrain evokes the empyrean with parallel risings of the moon on the front and back covers. This may have been his final design.

☖ 25 ☗

Guillaume Apollinaire. *Calligrammes: Poèmes de la paix et de la guerre (1913–1916)*. Paris: Mercure de France, 1918. 208 pages. Copy number 4 of 4 on Japon ancien; with an original etching by Pablo Picasso engraved by René Jaudon, and an original drawing by René Jaudon. Design: Rose Adler, 1925.

Despite the rigorous architecture of this fascinating binding for Apollinaire's *Calligrammes*, Adler showed early on the visual sensuality that would be characteristic of her style.

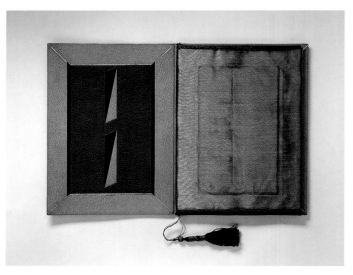

⬐ 26 ⬏

Stéphane Mallarmé. *L'Après-midi d'un faune*. Illustrated by Edouard Manet. Paris: Alphonse Derenne, 1876. 16 pages. Copy number 16 of 20 on Japon, with a watercolor wash on the tail piece and signed under the ex libris by Stéphane Mallarmé, to which a second copy of 16 pages on Hollande has been added. Autograph presentation inscription from Stéphane Mallarmé to Henri de Lapommeraye. Design: Rose Adler, 1925.

Not wanting to encroach on the achievement of Mallarmé and Manet, Adler decided to use a structurally simple case for *L'Après-midi d'un faune*. In the decoration, she creates a dream architecture, the ellipse of a city or a stellar choreography. At this early stage of her work, the interior is already equal artistically to the exterior.

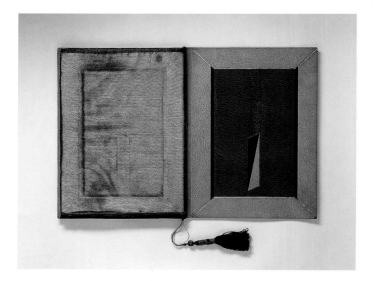

⊻ 27 ⊼

Pierre Reverdy. *Les Ardoises du toit*. Illustrated by Georges Braque. Paris, 1918. Copy number 1 of 5 on Japon impérial. Autograph presentation inscription from Pierre Reverdy to Jacques Doucet. Design: Rose Adler, 1925.

With restrained daring and a musical touch, Adler creates an exceptional work for Reverdy, offering a scattering of colored lozenges of astonishing modernity. On the spine, the heavily delineated title in the Japanese style is an homage to Art Nouveau, a detail all the more remarkable on a manifesto of Art Deco bookbinding.

⇘ 28 ⇙

Louis Aragon. *Les Aventures de Télémaque*. Paris: Editions de la Nouvelle Revue Française, 1922. 100 pages. Copy lettered D/O on Japon impérial; with a wide-margined proof of the portrait of the author by Robert Delaunay. Design: Rose Adler, 1925.

Similar to the binding for *Les Ardoises du toit*, this one features the same play of restraint and preciosity. The spine presents a pastiche of the art of lacquer (gold and red) and tips the work in the direction of oriental spareness. This is another sumptuously realized manifesto of Art Deco artistry.

↘ 29 ↙

Paul Valéry. *Eupalinos, ou l'architecte; precédé de L'Ame et la danse*. Paris: Editions de la Nouvelle Revue Française, 1923. 144 pages. Copy number 23 of 30 on Japon impérial. Design: Rose Adler, 1927.

The large format used for this binding is unusual for Adler. It is nonetheless similar to a series of small wrappers that form in her work a coherent expression of various Art Deco ideas. A lyricism and lightness lie behind the solidly displayed construction—a perfect homage to the spirit that Joseph Maria Olbrich displayed in his Viennese Secession Pavilion.

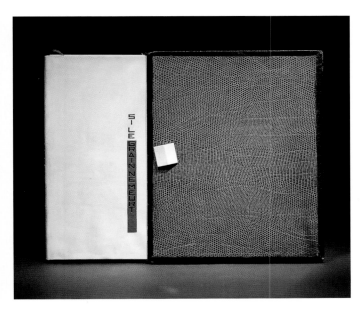

André Gide. *Si le grain ne meurt*. Paris: Edouard Champion, 1924. 42 leaves. Facsimile (collotype by Daniel Jacomet) of a fragment of the manuscript. Design: Rose Adler, 1927.

The simple, beautifully executed designs of the covers (shown here protruding from the slipcases) for these two facsimile editions embody the quintessence of a period and of its art. The splendid slipcases, of, respectively, lizard and snakeskin, and the buttons made of Galalith are among Adler's subtle variations.

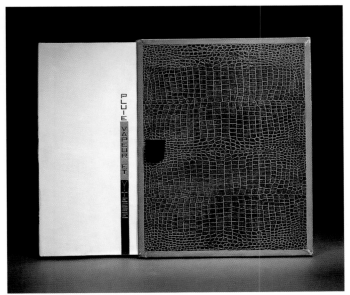

Paul Morand. *Pluie vapeur et vitesse*. Paris: Edouard Champion, 1926. 28 leaves of different sizes. Facsimile edition (collotype by Daniel Jacomet) of the manuscript. Design: Rose Adler, 1927.

Michel Leiris. *Simulacre.* **Illustrated by André Masson. Paris: Editions de la Galerie Simon, 1925. 36 pages. Copy number 5 of 10 on Japon ancien des Manufactures impériales. Design: Rose Adler, 1927.**

This is an immense binding, comparable to Legrain's for *Tête d'or* (no. 16). Adler's composition here reaches beyond mere fluency to achieve the clarity of a gesture. The perfection of form and of matter seems unsurpassable.

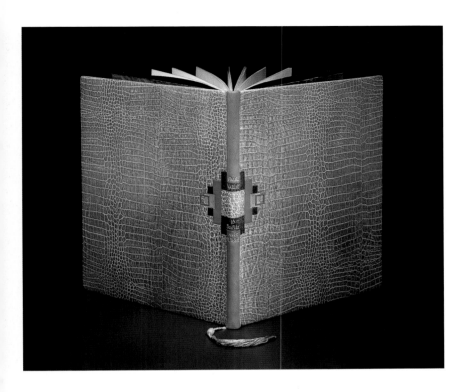

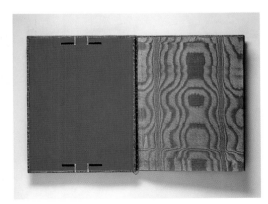

≫ 33 ≪
Paul Valéry. *La Soirée avec M. Teste*. Paris: Editions de la Nouvelle Revue Française, 1919. 28 pages. Copy number III of 3 on Tapestry-Strathmore. Design: Rose Adler, 1927.

With this binding, Adler shows us a different side of Art Deco from the one she displayed in *Simulacre*. By mimicking a clasp in the center and clips on the turn-ins, she plays with illusion and raises to a new level the beauty and refinement of the era.

Paul Morand. *Ouvert la nuit*. Paris: Editions de la Nouvelle Revue Française, 1922. 200 pages. Copy reimposed for printing on vergé pur fil de Lafuma-Navarre, printed for Jacques Doucet. Design: Rose Adler, 1928.

By means of an undulation and the sky seen through a lunette, simplicity and preciosity strengthen each other on this binding for Morand's *Ouvert la nuit*. The second phase of Art Deco—pure melody—has arrived.

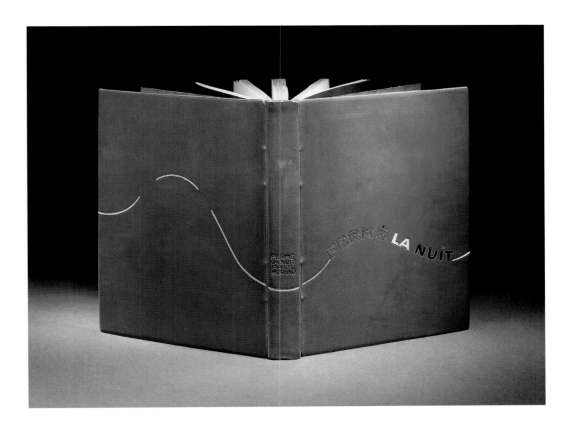

⤦ 35 ⤧

Paul Morand. *Fermé la nuit*. Paris: Editions de la Nouvelle Revue Française, 1923. 212 pages. Copy reimposed for printing on vergé pur fil de Lafuma-Navarre, printed for Jacques Doucet. Design: Rose Adler, 1928.

More restrained than its pendant in the Morand diptych, this binding can be summed up as a slow, hesitating curve. Here, in homage to the title, Adler confines herself to essentials.

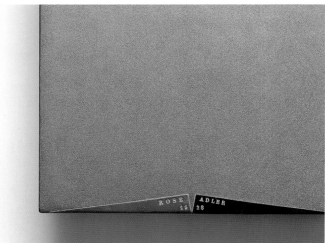

Louis Aragon. *Le Paysan de Paris*. Paris: Editions de la Nouvelle Revue Française, 1926. 256 pages. Copy reimposed for printing on vergé pur fil de Lafuma-Navarre, printed for Jacques Doucet. Design: Rose Adler, 1928.

Aragon, like Morand, was a favorite of Adler's. Here she combines opposites, both in terms of the leather and of the different placement of the clips on the simulated clasp. Diverse colors and materials blend to achieve an overall elegance.

Paul Morand. *Poèmes*. **Paris: Au Sans Pareil, 1924. 144 pages. Copy number 23 of 30 on Japon ancien. Design: Rose Adler, 1928.**

For Morand's *Poèmes*, Adler converts the power of a monumental skyscraper to a sign of improbable weightlessness. This tour de force from the second phase of Art Deco blends the simple with the mannered.

POEMES
PAUL
MORAND

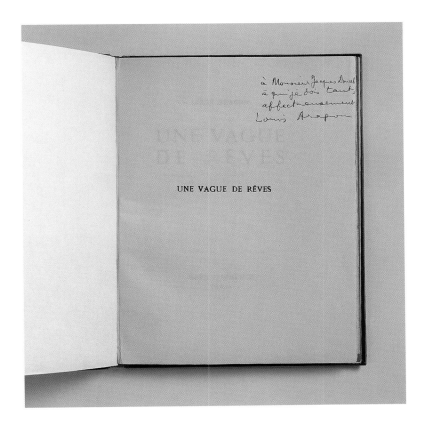

UNE VAGUE DE RÊVES

**Louis Aragon. *Une Vague de rêves*. Paris, 1924.
Copy hors commerce. 40 pages. Autograph
presentation inscription from Louis Aragon to
Jacques Doucet. Design: Rose Adler, 1929.**

This simple vellum binding exerts a magnetic
attraction. Inventiveness and subtlety are at their
peak here: the three concentric circles suggest
the ripples created when a stone is thrown
into water.

Raymond Roussel. *La Poussière de soleils*. Paris: Librairie Alphonse Lemerre, 1927. 240 pages. Printed on Grand Papier Japon; extra-illustrated with 17 color reproductions. A 12-page brochure, *La Critique et l'auteur de "La Poussière de soleils,"* has been inserted into this copy. Autograph presentation inscription from Raymond Roussel to Jacques Doucet. Design: Rose Adler, 1929.

As imposing as Legrain's binding for *La Ville* (no. 15), this one by Adler is striking for the tension that animates it. The light dusting of gold dots has an evanescence that seems to grasp all things.

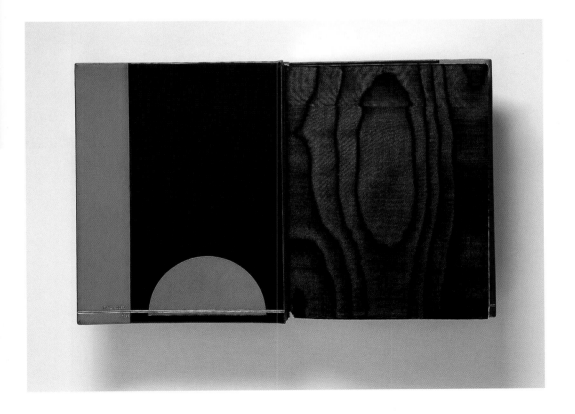

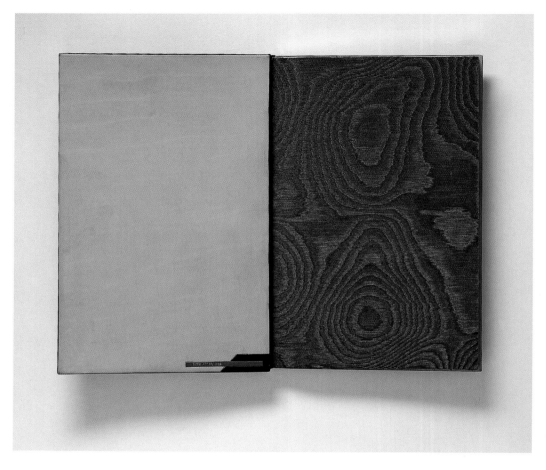

⬎ 40 ⬐

**Auguste de Villiers de L'Isle-Adam. *Trois contes
cruels*. Illustrated by Jean-Emile Laboureur. Paris:
Aux dépens de la Société de la Gravure sur
bois originale, 1927. 52 pages. Artist's copy
(lettered J). Design: Rose Adler, 1929.**

An eloquent but enigmatic binding, this composition serves as a refutation of the Jansenist and
geometrical focus of the first period of Art Deco.
The unfolding of time that is evoked is also that
of the book.

Colette. *L'Envers du Music-Hall.* **Illustrated by Jean-Emile Laboureur. Paris: Au Sans Pareil, 1926. 176 pages. Printed on vergé de Rives. Design: Rose Adler, 1929.**

With virtuosity and an orchestration of movement and materials, Adler created this binding as a suggestive homage to Paris nights and the feminine leg. Inside, the unusual appearance of Jacques Doucet's initials signals the end of an era.

↘ 42 ↙

**Francis de Croisset. *Aux fêtes de Kapurthala*.
Paris: Les Editions Kra, 1929. 64 pages. Printed on
vélin. Autograph letters to Jacques Doucet from
Henri-Pierre Roché and from the Maharajah of
Kapurthala, tipped in. Design: Rose Adler, 1930.**

A great artistic achievement and a magnificent state-
ment (as was Legrain's binding for *Les Amis nouveaux*
[no. 22]), this binding justifies Rose Adler's ambition,
which was to create an object both jewel-like and
imposing, despite the small format.

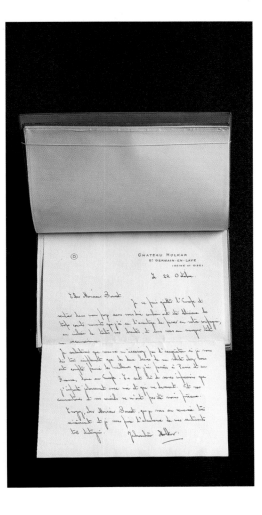

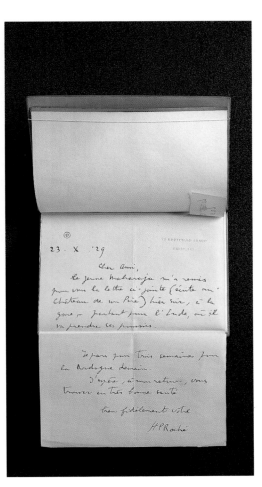

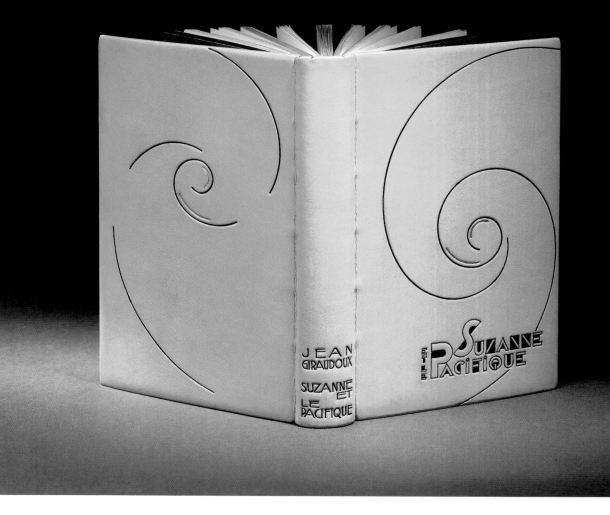

〜 43 〜

Jean Giraudoux. *Suzanne et le Pacifique*. Paris: Emile-Paul Frères Editeurs, 1921. 300 pages. Copy number 7 of 15 on Japon; extra-illustrated with six drypoint engravings by Denise Bernollin (each limited to 10 copies and executed at the request of Jacques Doucet as a loose suite of illustrations for Jean Giraudoux's story). Design: Rose Adler, 1930.

For Giraudoux's *Suzanne et le Pacifique*, Adler conceived, between purity and excess, the path of a curve becoming a spiral and integrating the design of the title.

Tristan Bernard. *Tableau de la boxe*. Illustrated by André Dunoyer de Segonzac. Paris: Editions de la Nouvelle Revue Française, 1922. Copy number 282 of 318 on vélin; the paper covers bound in. Design: Rose Adler, 1931.

The polished squares on the front and back covers mimic a boxing ring—an understated triumph by Adler at her prime.

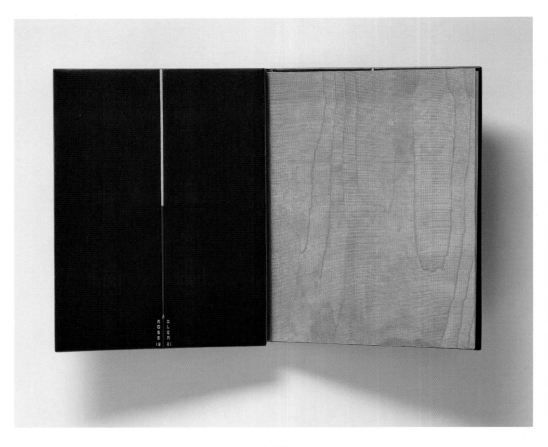

⤊ 45 ⤉
Pierre Louÿs. *Maddalou*. Illustrated by Edouard Degaine. Paris: Les Editions Briant-Robert, 1927. 48 pages. Printed on vélin d'Arches. Design: Rose Adler, 1931.

For the binding for Louÿs's *Maddalou*, Adler tackled emptiness and plenitude, implicating the title in the piece's excess and offering homages here to Legrain and there to Doucet, who had both died in 1929. This binding proclaims a new style as much as it closes the door on an adventure.

Dimensions of the closed books, in centimeters, are height by width. Entries in the catalogue raisonné *Pierre Legrain relieur: Répertoire descriptif et bibliographique de mille deux cent trente-six reliures* (Paris: Auguste Blaizot for the Société de la Reliure originale, 1965) are designated by the prefix *PLR*.

Bindings by Pierre Legrain

1 (p. 40)

Blaise Cendrars. *Les Pâques*. Paris: Les Hommes nouveaux, 1912. 16 pages. With a preliminary line drawing, in red, by the author. Autograph presentation inscription from Blaise Cendrars to Isabelle Bender. Autograph letters from Blaise Cendrars and Isabelle Bender to Jacques Doucet, tipped in.

Matte black paper binding over boards. Centered on each cover is a vellum roundel, framed with a gilt fillet. At the foot of the front cover, the author's name and the title, gilt, on a horizontal strip of black hard-grained leather. At the foot of the spine, a vertical strip of black hard-grained leather carries the author's name in gilt letters, cascading singly down the spine. Pastedowns and endleaves of gold paper. 21.5 x 13.5 cm.

1917. Signed and designed by Pierre Legrain for Jacques Doucet. Executed by Germaine Schroeder.

Bibliothèque littéraire Jacques Doucet, C-VII-22. *PLR* 130.

2 (p. 41)

Paul Claudel. *Corona Benignitatis Anni Dei*. Paris: Editions de la Nouvelle Revue Française, 1915. 248 pages. Copy number 47 of 75, with the text reimposed for printing on pur fil Voiron.

Golden-tan goatskin binding. Each cover carries four vertical bands of black goatskin framed within thick gilt fillets, with the same design carried onto the spine. At the center of the spine, the band of black goatskin broadens into a lozenge, which serves as a label with the title worked horizontally in gilt letters; the foot of the spine ends in a rectangular black goatskin label with the author's name in gilt letters. Turn-ins of golden-tan goatskin, decorated with a thick gilt fillet; doublures and endleaves of brown faille; second endleaves of Doucet wallpaper with vertical bands of white, black, and gold. 22 x 16.5 cm. Slipcased.

1917. Signed and designed by Pierre Legrain for Jacques Doucet. Executed by Henri Noulhac.

Bibliothèque littéraire Jacques Doucet, C-VIII-22. *PLR* 157.

3 (pp. 42–43)

Blaise Cendrars. *Profond aujourd'hui*. Illustrated by Angel Zarraga. Paris: A la belle Edition, 1917. 48 pages. Copy number 1 of 5 on Chine, the gatherings variously folded; with a suite of five drawings (without colored highlights) and one original finished drawing.

Three-quarter binding of handmade paper in green, silver, and pink, with vertical vellum strips. On the front cover, between the vellum strips, two pieces of black goatskin, set within gilt swelled rules, bearing the title in gilt letters. These goatskin elements are repeated on the spine and on the outer vellum strips, as though laced across the boards and through the spine. On the spine, the author's name tooled in gilt letters cascading singly down the back. The linings, both doublure and endleaves, of matte black paper. 21.5 x 13.5 cm.

1917. Signed and designed by Pierre Legrain for Jacques Doucet. Executed by René Kieffer.

Bibliothèque littéraire Jacques Doucet, C-VII-25. *PLR* 131.

4 (p. 44)

Remy de Gourmont. *Couleurs* [contes nouveaux suivis de *Choses anciennes*]. Paris: Mercure de France, 1908. 248 pages. Copy number 4 of 15 on Hollande.

Orange goatskin binding. Toward the foot of the covers and the spine, a horizontal swelled ribbon of black goatskin traverses the expanse, the two contracted sections on each cover connecting over a silver roundel, the black goatskin tooled with three vertical rules in silver. On the spine, the ribbon is interrupted by the orange goatskin that emerges as a mauve-bordered goatskin titling-label, tooled in silver, and surrounded by a thick and a thin silver fillet; the author's name is tooled in silver at the foot. Turn-ins of orange and black goatskin, decorated in beige goatskin, with a thick and a thin silver fillet; black doublures and endleaves; second endleaves of paper with black, white, and gold stripes. 19.5 x 13 cm. Slipcased.

The design for the ribbon is in Legrain's album of designs in The New York Public Library's Spencer Collection (Spencer Mss. 185).

1917. Signed and designed by Pierre Legrain for Jacques Doucet. Executed by René Kieffer.

Bibliothèque littéraire Jacques Doucet, E-VII-6. *PLR* 424.

5 (p. 44)

Remy de Gourmont. *Divertissements*. Paris: Georges Crès, 1912. 180 pages.

Black goatskin binding. Toward the foot of the covers and the spine, a horizontal ribbon of beige goatskin traverses the expanse, the sections on each cover overlaid with two strips of black goatskin, all framed in silver. On the spine, the title tooled in silver on the beige band, with the author's name in silver at the foot. Turn-ins of black goatskin, decorated in beige goatskin, with a thick and a thin silver fillet; doublures and endleaves of silver lamé; second endleaves of paper with black, white, and gold stripes. 19.5 x 13 cm. Slipcased.

1917. Signed and designed by Pierre Legrain for Jacques Doucet. Executed by René Kieffer.

Bibliothèque littéraire Jacques Doucet, E-VII-9. *PLR* 427.

6 (p. 45)

Remy de Gourmont. *Les Chevaux de Diomède*. Paris: Mercure de France, 1897. 256 pages. Copy number 2 of 3 on Japon impérial.

Carmine-red goatskin binding. Toward the foot of the covers and the spine, a horizontal ribbon of black goatskin undulates across the entire expanse, each undulation marked with a circle of black goatskin enclosing a gilt fillet through whose center the red shows. The rhythm is interrupted at the spine by a black goatskin roundel on which the title of the work is tooled in gilt letters; below this label, the author's name is tooled in gilt letters at the foot of the spine. Turn-ins of carmine-red goatskin, decorated in black goatskin, with a thick and a thin gilt fillet; doublures and endleaves of black taffeta; second endleaves of red marbled paper. 20 x 15.5 cm. Slipcased.

1917. Signed and designed by Pierre Legrain for Jacques Doucet. Executed by René Kieffer.

Bibliothèque littéraire Jacques Doucet, E-VI-17. *PLR* 423.

7 (p. 46)

Jean de Tinan. *L'Exemple de Ninon de L'Enclos amoureuse*. Paris: Mercure de France, 1898. 216 pages. Copy A of copies lettered A–Z, on Chine.

Blonde calf binding. An interrupted, angled band of black goatskin traverses the covers and spine, anchored at the center of each cover by a large roundel outlined with single gilt tools. Within the roundel on the front cover, the author's name is tooled in gilt letters toward the bottom of the inner arc; the roundel on the rear cover is blank. The black goatskin section of the spine, with gilt tooling at the top and bottom edges on the blonde calf, constitutes a label bearing the complete title in single gilt letters worked horizontally. Turn-ins of blonde calf, decorated with gilt single tools and the continuation of the black goatskin band; doublures and endleaves of black faille; second endleaves of paper marbled ocher and green. 19 x 11.5 cm. Slipcased.

1917. Signed and designed by Pierre Legrain for Jacques Doucet. Executed by René Kieffer.

Bibliothèque littéraire Jacques Doucet, H-VI-6. *PLR* 995.

8 (p. 47)

Paul Claudel. *Partage de midi*. Paris: Bibliothèque de l'Occident, 1906. 156 pages. Copy hors commerce.

Blue-green goatskin binding. An overall design of five concentric circles in blind, each with an interior appliqué of a black goatskin roundel framed by a thick green goatskin border framed in gold. The circle across the lower part of the spine, the circumference contracted at its top into a chevron, is tooled in gilt with the title and the author's name at the foot. Turn-ins of blue-green goatskin, decorated with a thick gilt fillet on which the cover design is mimicked; doublures and endleaves of black faille; second endleaves of paper marbled blue-green and pink. 26 x 17 cm. Slipcased.

1917. Signed and designed by Pierre Legrain for Jacques Doucet. Executed by René Kieffer.

Bibliothèque littéraire Jacques Doucet, C-VIII-11. *PLR* 165.

9 (pp. 48–49)

André Gide. *Les Cahiers d'André Walter*. Corrected proofs for the published edition of 1891. Paris: Librairie de l'Art indépendant. 256 pages.

Dark-brown goatskin binding. On each cover, a stylized hand-mirror created from curved gilt fillets. The spine alludes to the cover design; at the head, a rectangular titling label tooled in gilt with single letters for the author's first initial and last name; at the foot, the title in gilt letters. The turn-ins a border of dark-brown goatskin, decorated at head and foot with a straight double-gilt fillet, and at the edge of the inner margin with a curved double-gilt fillet; doublure and endleaf of black faille; second set of endleaves of brown, green, and russet marbled paper. 17.2 x 12.5 cm. Slipcased.

1917. Signed and designed by Pierre Legrain for Jacques Doucet. Executed by René Kieffer.

Bibliothèque littéraire Jacques Doucet, B-VI-16. *PLR* 356.

10 (p. 50)

Paul Verlaine. *Les Poètes maudits*. Paris: Léon Vanier, 1884. 58 pages.

Brown-violet hard-grained leather binding. On the inner edge of the covers, two rectangular vertical pieces of black goatskin, extended by a single tool in silver, and counterposed. Along the spine, between a third set of the same rectangular elements, the author's name and the title tooled horizontally in gilt letters. The turn-ins a border of brown-violet hard-grained leather, decorated with a slender silver fillet rendered double at the top and the bottom by a thick silver fillet; doublure and endleaf of black faille, with second endleaves of handmade paper colored brown, green, coral, and silver. 19 x 11.5 cm. Slipcased.

1918. Signed and designed by Pierre Legrain for Jacques Doucet. Executed by René Kieffer.

Bibliothèque littéraire Jacques Doucet, H-VIII-8. *PLR* 1164.

11 (p. 51)
André Gide. *Feuilles de route, 1895–1896.* Brussels: Imprimerie N. Vandersypen, 1899. 76 pages. Autograph presentation inscription from André Gide to Henry D. Davray.

Polished brown calf binding. On the front cover, gilt fillets suggest stacked leaves (i.e., *feuilles*) above the title in gilt letters. The author's last name in gilt letters at the foot of the spine. The turn-ins a border of polished brown calf, with four gilt fillets alluding to the design on the front cover; doublure and endleaf of black moiré taffeta, with second endleaves of brown, red, and gold paper. 15 x 11 cm. Slipcased.

1917. Signed and designed by Pierre Legrain for Jacques Doucet. Executed by Henri Noulhac.

Bibliothèque littéraire Jacques Doucet, D-VIII-5. *PLR* 361.

12 (p. 52)
André Gide. *Lettres à Angèle, 1898–1899.* Paris: Mercure de France, 1900. 170 pages. Printed on Hollande. Autograph presentation inscription from André Gide to Louis Dumur.

Vellum binding. On the covers and spine, a deep-brown calf border, outlined by a thick gilt fillet, with a thin vertical strip of green hard-grained leather like a place-marker. On the front cover and across the spine, the author's first initial, his last name, and the title of the work in gilt letters. The turn-ins a border of deep-brown calf, decorated with a thick gilt fillet; doublure and endleaves of brown faille, second endleaves of yellow and beige marbled paper. 15 x 11.5 cm. Slipcased.

1918. Signed and designed by Pierre Legrain for Jacques Doucet. Executed by Henri Noulhac.

Bibliothèque littéraire Jacques Doucet, D-VIII-7. *PLR* 369.

13 (p. 53)
Guillaume Apollinaire. *L'Hérésiarque et Cie.* Paris: P.-V. Stock, 1910. 288 pages. Copy number 8 of 21 on Hollande.

Bright pink goatskin binding. At the bottom of the front cover is a large letter "H" in black goatskin extending from one edge of the binding to the other, and onto the turn-ins; on each side of this "H" are the other letters of the title in gilt tooling. On the spine, the name of the author in gilt letters. The turn-ins a border of bright pink goatskin embellished with a thick gilt fillet; doublures and endleaves of gold paper. 19.5 x 13.5 cm. Slipcased.

1918. Signed and designed by Pierre Legrain for Jacques Doucet. Executed by René Kieffer.

Bibliothèque littéraire Jacques Doucet, C-V-6. *PLR* 16.

14 (pp. 54–55)
André Gide. *L'Immoraliste.* Manuscript. 225 leaves.

Citron goatskin binding. At the head and the foot of each cover and across the spine, an inward-curving strip of black goatskin, edged in blue goatskin. On the front cover, the title worked in large letters of black goatskin. On the spine, a titling-label of blue goatskin, the author's name worked in silver letters cascading singly down the back. The turn-ins a border of citron goatskin decorated with black and blue goatskin and with three silver fillets worked vertically; doublure and endleaves of black taffeta; second set of endleaves of yellow and blue marbled paper. 34.5 x 24 cm. Slipcased.

1918. Signed and designed by Pierre Legrain for Jacques Doucet. Executed by René Kieffer.

Bibliothèque littéraire Jacques Doucet, B-V-25. *PLR* 362.

15 (p. 56)

Paul Claudel. *La Ville*. Manuscript. 131 leaves.

Olive-green goatskin binding. The covers and spine edged with a single gilt tool, interrupted by the joint. On the spine, the title worked in gilt letters cascading singly down the back; the author's name tooled in gilt letters. The turn-ins a border of olive goatskin decorated with a continuation of the gilt tool; doublure and endleaves of alternating gray and mauve taffeta; second set of endleaves of gray, green, and pink marbled paper. 28.5 x 23.5 cm. Slipcased.

1918. Signed and designed by Pierre Legrain for Jacques Doucet. Executed by Georges Canape.

Bibliothèque littéraire Jacques Doucet, B-V-17. *PLR* 172.

16 (p. 57)

Paul Claudel. *Tête d'or*. Manuscript in two hands, a copyist's and the author's. 280 leaves.

Deep-brown goatskin binding. Inset into each cover, a rectangular panel of beige sharkskin. On the spine, the title worked in letters cascading singly down the back, each letter imposed in deep-brown goatskin on a gilt roundel; the word *Poésie*, the author's name, and the citation *Manuscrit* in blind. The turn-ins a border of deep-brown goatskin decorated with gilt roundels; doublure and endleaves of gold lamé; second set of endleaves of black and gold marbled paper. 28.5 x 23.5 cm. Slipcased.

1918. Signed and designed by Pierre Legrain for Jacques Doucet. Executed by Georges Canape.

Bibliothèque littéraire Jacques Doucet, B-V-18. *PLR* 169.

17 (pp. 58–59)

Guillaume Apollinaire. *Le Poète assassiné*. Manuscript. 153 leaves.

Black goatskin binding. At the center of the front cover, a rectangular panel in red goatskin with short cross arms framed in a broad gilt border, and, adjoining both on the left and on the right, two square sections of red goatskin. The title is tooled horizontally in gilt letters on the horizontal central portion and in black goatskin on the square pieces of red goatskin. The spine bears two square panels in red goatskin, lettered horizontally with, respectively, the author's name and the title. The back cover carries a blank version of the broken-rectangular red panel within the broad gilt border. The turn-ins a border of black goatskin decorated with a thick gilt fillet; doublure and endleaves of black watered silk; second set of endleaves of pink and gold paper. 33 x 23.5 cm. Slipcased.

1918. Signed and designed by Pierre Legrain for Jacques Doucet. Executed by René Kieffer.

Bibliothèque littéraire Jacques Doucet, B-V-5. *PLR* 19.

18 (p. 60)

André Suarès. *Les Bourdons sont en fleurs*. Manuscript. 48 leaves.

Dusty-rose goatskin binding. Corners of black goatskin, with gilt inserts, continuing across the spine. At the center of the front cover, the title in gilt letters, each letter in a roundel of black goatskin and all framing a central motif of irregularly shaped roundels in dusty rose, rising out of a background of a gilt hexagon. The spine is blank. The turn-ins a border of dusty-rose goatskin decorated with black goatskin with gilt inserts; doublure and endleaves of black watered silk; second set of endleaves of paper with a frothy finish in pink, green, and yellow. 21.8 x 17.5 cm. Slipcased.

1918. Designed by Pierre Legrain for Jacques Doucet. Executed by Georges Canape.

Bibliothèque littéraire Jacques Doucet, B-VII-9. *PLR* 920.

19 (p. 61)

André Gide. *Le Voyage d'Urien*. Illustrated by Maurice Denis. Paris: Librairie de l'Art indépendant, 1893. 102 pages. A suite of lithographs by Maurice Denis, proof before letters, without the text. Printed on Japon.

Black goatskin binding. On the front cover, the title in gilt letters within interlaces of red goatskin, connected by single gilt tools in a lozenge, continuing across the spine, the back cover, and the linings. The spine carries the author's first initial and last name tooled in gilt letters cascading singly down the back. Turn-ins of black goatskin decorated by a gilt fillet and by fillets of red goatskin; doublure and endleaves of black taffeta; second endleaves of mauve marbled paper. 21 x 19 cm. Slipcased.

1919. Signed and designed by Pierre Legrain for Jacques Doucet. Executed by Georges Canape.

Bibliothèque littéraire Jacques Doucet, D-VII-27. *PLR* 395.

20 (p. 62)

Jean Paulhan. *Le Guerrier appliqué*. Manuscript. 247 leaves.

.Vellum portfolio with wallet-edged flaps of black goatskin decorated with a gilt fillet. Along the spine, a rectangular black goatskin titling label decorated with a thick gilt fillet and folding down over the covers; title in gilt letters; at the foot of the spine, a triangular piece of black goatskin, decorated with thick gilt fillets bearing the author's name. Doublure of alternating pink and yellow silk. 11 x 13.5 cm. Slipcased.

1920. Signed and designed by Pierre Legrain for Jacques Doucet. Executed by Henri Noulhac.

Bibliothèque littéraire Jacques Doucet, B-VI-21. *PLR* 756.

21 (p. 63)

Paul Valéry. *Charmes*. Manuscript. 69 leaves.

Elephant-gray goatskin binding. In the center of each cover an aluminum-tooled disk bearing the stylized head of a cat. On the spine, the title, the author's name, and the word *Manuscrit* in aluminum letters. The turn-ins a border of elephant-gray goatskin, embellished with a thin double fillet of aluminum, framing a thick gilt fillet; doublure and endleaves of black faille; second endleaves of Koch handmade paper in pink, gray, and gold. 27 x 23 cm. Slipcased.

1923. Signed and designed by Pierre Legrain for Jacques Doucet. Executed by René Kieffer.

Bibliothèque littéraire Jacques Doucet, B-V-12. *PLR* 1021.

22 (pp. 64–65)

Paul Morand. *Les Amis nouveaux*. Illustrated by Jean Hugo. Paris: Au Sans Pareil, 1924. 40 pages. Copy number 21 of 30 on Japon impérial; with a suite of nine drypoints with watercolor.

Blue calf binding, sheathed in a perforated half-binding of nickel. In each perforation, the calf is stamped with a gilt dot; the title is engraved on the nickel of the front cover. On the spine, three fillets of gilt vertical dots, interrupted to show the title and the author's name in gilt letters. Turn-ins of blue calf, half decorated with a single blind-tooled fillet, and half with double fillets of gilt dots; doublures and endleaves of midnight-blue watered silk; two rivets of chromed steel on each inner margin; second endleaves of paper marbled green, blue, gold, and beige. 20 x 14 cm.

1927. Signed and designed by Pierre Legrain for Jacques Doucet.

Bibliothèque littéraire Jacques Doucet, F-VIII-26. *PLR* 711.

23 (pp. 66–67)

André Salmon. *Le Calumet*. Paris: Henri Falque, 1910. 132 pages. Copy number 6 of 20 on Hollande. Autograph presentation inscription from André Salmon to Jacques Doucet.

Black goatskin binding. On the top and bottom of the covers and spine, a thick aluminum fillet interrupted in the center of the covers and on the joints; at the bottom of the front cover, disks of green goatskin radiate over and around a black goatskin disk on which the title is tooled in aluminum letters. On the spine, the title and author's name in aluminum letters. The turn-ins a border of black goatskin, decorated with a gilt fillet and patterned in green goatskin on which the thick aluminum fillet is prolonged over the covers; doublure and endleaves of green faille; second endleaves of glazed paper marbled green and gold. 19.5 x 13.5 cm. Slipcased.

The design for the front cover is in Legrain's album of designs in The New York Public Library's Spencer Collection (Spencer Mss. 185).

1928. SIGNED AND DESIGNED BY PIERRE LEGRAIN FOR JACQUES DOUCET.

Bibliothèque littéraire Jacques Doucet, G-VI-24. *PLR* 891.

24 (p. 68)

Georges Rouault. *Paysages légendaires*. Paris: Editions Porteret, 1929. Copy number 6 of 165; with a suite of eight original lithographs (two retouched), hand-colored by the author.

Brown goatskin binding. At the foot of each cover, a curved expanse of black goatskin, opening upward, out of which rises an appliquéd roundel symbolizing the rising moon. The roundel on the front cover is tooled in a sunburst pattern with radiating dotted lines in silver, with the title tooled in single letters in blind, the outside letters within a blind-tooled square border. The roundel is repeated, without letters, on the back cover, where the design continues. Above the roundel on both covers, a semé of single tools

depicts a stylized version of the heavens, the firmament depicted by a regular scattering of gilt stars and silver dots. The spine, below five gilt stars, ends in a titling label of black goatskin, bearing the author's name and the title in horizontal lines of single letters tooled alternately in silver and gilt. Turn-ins of brown goatskin, ruled in blind with a regular pattern of gilt stars in the border, above a continuation of the black goatskin; doublures and endleaves of pale-gray suede; second endleaves of paper marbled brown, maroon, orange, and green. 33.5 x 26 cm. Slipcased.

1929. SIGNED AND DESIGNED BY PIERRE LEGRAIN.

The New York Public Library, Spencer Collection, French 1929. *PLR* LXVIII.

Bindings by Rose Adler

25 (pp. 72–73)

Guillaume Apollinaire. *Calligrammes: Poèmes de la paix et de la guerre (1913–1916)*. Paris: Mercure de France, 1918. 208 pages. Copy number 4 of 4 on Japon ancien; with an original etching by Pablo Picasso engraved by René Jaudon, and an original drawing by René Jaudon.

Ivory calf binding. On each cover a large beige pattern inlaid with black calf, set within two fillets, one thick and aluminum, the other thin and tooled in gilt. On the front cover, the title in aluminum letters occupying the inlay of black calf and overlapping onto the inlay of beige goatskin. On the spine, an overlapping of black calf; three new inlays of black calf for the title and the author's name, each enhanced with a roundel of black calf stamped with an aluminum dot. Aluminum edges. The turn-ins a border of black calf, embellished with thick aluminum fillets, inlay of a rectangular panel of black calf with a mosaic of beige goatskin (different on the front and on the back); endleaves of silver lamé; second endleaves of Langrand handmade paper. 23 x 13.9 cm. Wrapper and slipcase of aluminum paper framed by red and black calf; spine in black calf, the title and the author's name in aluminum letters on three inlays of beige goatskin, each one enhanced by a roundel of beige goatskin including a dot made of red calf.

1925. Signed and designed by Rose Adler for Jacques Doucet. Executed by Adolphe Cuzin.

Bibliothèque littéraire Jacques Doucet, C-V-12.

26 (pp. 74–75)

Stéphane Mallarmé. *L'Après-midi d'un faune*. Illustrated by Edouard Manet. Paris: Alphonse Derenne, 1876. 16 pages. Copy number 16 of 20 on Japon, with a watercolor wash on the tail piece and signed under the ex libris by Stéphane Mallarmé, to which a second copy of 16 pages on Hollande has been added. Autograph presentation inscription from Stéphane Mallarmé to Henri de Lapommeraye.

Natural goatskin portfolio. On each cover, segments of lizard and a mosaic of black and jade-green goatskin, dotted with full aluminum tooling. On the spine, the title in aluminum enhanced with an inlay of jade-green goatskin, tooled in aluminum. The turn-ins a border of natural goatskin, embellished with thick aluminum fillets, inlay of a jade-green rectangular panel patterned in natural and black goatskin (each cover different from the other); endleaves of silver lamé, framed by a band of black goatskin on the top, and by a double band of jade-green and black goatskin at the bottom; second endleaves of jade-green glazed paper. With a tassel of black thread. 31.5 x 22.4 cm. Slipcase of gray wood veneer bordered with jade-green and black goatskin and lizard.

1925. Signed and designed by Rose Adler for Jacques Doucet. Executed by Adolphe Cuzin.

Bibliothèque littéraire Jacques Doucet, E-IV-12.

27 (p. 76)

Pierre Reverdy. *Les Ardoises du toit*. Illustrated by Georges Braque. Paris, 1918. Copy number 1 of 5 on Japon impérial. Autograph presentation inscription from Pierre Reverdy to Jacques Doucet.

Beige hard-grained leather binding. On each cover, a patterned dotting of roundels in ivory, citron, and flame-colored hard-grained leather, with black added to the back cover. Spine of ivory hard-grained leather, mottled in hard-grained leather in citron and black with the letters of the title cascading singly down the spine in black and silver; black hard-grained leather simulated fasteners overlapping onto the covers. Silver edges. The turn-ins a border of beige hard-grained leather embellished with a silver fillet, inlay of a rectangular panel of vellum enhanced by a double fillet of orange and citron goatskin; endleaves of silver lamé; second endleaves of handmade gray and gold paper. 19.5 x 13.8 cm. Wrapper and slipcase of citron goatskin and silver embossed paper, the spine of citron goatskin repeating the color of the binding, the title in blind with the author's name.

1925. Signed and designed by Rose Adler for Jacques Doucet. Executed by Adolphe Cuzin.

Bibliothèque littéraire Jacques Doucet, G-VI-17.

28 (p. 77)

Louis Aragon. *Les Aventures de Télémaque*. Paris: Editions de la Nouvelle Revue Française, 1922. 100 pages. Copy lettered D/O on Japon impérial; with a wide-margined proof of the portrait of the author by Robert Delaunay.

Black calf binding. On each cover, a patterned dotting of roundels in ivory and red calf and green goatskin, and, on the back cover, the addition of single full-gilt roundels. Blank spine covered with gold leaf, simulated clasps patterned in lacquer-red calf. Gilt edges. The turn-ins a border of lacquer-red calf, intersected by gilt tooling at an angle, inlay of a rectangular panel of gold lamé heightened by a green fillet; endleaves of gold lamé; second endleaves of green and gold Roussy handmade paper. 16.2 x 12.3 cm. Wrapper and slipcase of Roussy handmade paper, edged in lacquer-red calf, the title and author's name in gilt letters on an inlay of green and lacquer-red goatskin.

1925. SIGNED AND DESIGNED BY ROSE ADLER FOR JACQUES DOUCET. EXECUTED BY ADOLPHE CUZIN.

Bibliothèque littéraire Jacques Doucet, C-V-16.

29 (p. 78)

Paul Valéry. *Eupalinos, ou l'architecte; precédé de L'Ame et la danse*. Paris: Editions de la Nouvelle Revue Française, 1923. 144 pages. Copy number 23 of 30 on Japon impérial.

Vellum binding. On the front cover, inlays of black crocodile and light-tan goatskin, intersected by full gilt tooling, and surrounded by fillets in gilt, in aluminum, and in blind. On the back cover, at the bottom, an inlay of a light-tan goatskin rectangle, the date of publication in gilt and enhanced by a full gilt tool. On the spine, a rectangle of black goatskin for part of the title, in gilt letters cascading down the spine, as well as a rectangle of light-tan goatskin displaying the author's last name tooled on the tail piece in gilt letters (his first name tooled above it on the vellum). Gilt edges. Doublure of light-tan goatskin; endleaves of black watered silk; second endleaves of red and gold paper. 32.8 x 24.6 cm. Wrapper with wallet-edged flaps and slipcase of black, silver, and gold paper, and of vellum.

1927. SIGNED AND DESIGNED BY ROSE ADLER FOR JACQUES DOUCET. EXECUTED BY EMMANUEL LECARPENTIER.

Bibliothèque littéraire Jacques Doucet, F-IV-31.

30 (p. 79)

André Gide. *Si le grain ne meurt*. Paris: Edouard Champion, 1924. 42 leaves. Facsimile (collotype by Daniel Jacomet) of a fragment of the manuscript.

Vellum portfolio lined with natural wood veneer. On the front cover, a patterned vertical band of green calf, the letters of the title cascading singly down, in blind, partially on the vellum and partially on the band of green calf. On the spine, a vertical band of patterned chamois calf, the author's name cascading down the spine, in blind, partially on the vellum and partially on the band of chamois calf. 24 x 19.6 cm. Slipcase of green lizard, bordered with black goatskin, ribbon tab with ivory-colored Galalith square pull.

1927. DESIGNED BY ROSE ADLER FOR JACQUES DOUCET.

Bibliothèque littéraire Jacques Doucet, A-VI-11.

31 (p. 79)

Paul Morand. *Pluie vapeur et vitesse*. Paris: Edouard Champion, 1926. 28 leaves of different sizes. Facsimile edition (collotype by Daniel Jacomet) of the manuscript.

Vellum portfolio lined in natural wood veneer. On the front cover, a patterned vertical band of black and mustard-yellow calf, the letters of the title cascading singly down, in gilt and in blind, partially on the vellum and partially on the band of black and mustard-yellow calf. On the spine, a vertical band of mustard-yellow calf, the author's name cascading down in blind, partially on the vellum and partially on the band of mustard-yellow calf. 27.2 x 21.2 cm. Slipcase of dark-gray snakeskin, bordered with mustard-yellow calf, ribbon tab with black Galalith square pull.

1927. DESIGNED BY ROSE ADLER FOR JACQUES DOUCET.

Bibliothèque littéraire Jacques Doucet, A-VI-9.

32 (p. 80)

Michel Leiris. *Simulacre*. Illustrated by André Masson. Paris: Editions de la Galerie Simon, 1925. 36 pages. Copy number 5 of 10 on Japon ancien des Manufactures impériales.

Black calf binding. On the front cover, on center, inlay of a cabochon of agate, crowning a semi-oval in coral-pink crocodile, set within an aluminum fillet. On the spine, a mosaic of red calf at the bottom, the letters of the title cascading singly down, in aluminum on the black calf and in black on the red calf. Aluminum edges. Full leather doublure lacquered in gilt; endleaves of black watered silk; second endleaves of handmade black and silver paper. 25.8 x 19.4 cm. Wrapper and slipcase of silver paper with red highlights, bordered in black calf; on the spine, the author's name, the letters cascading singly down, in black on a band of silver paper bordered in black calf.

1927. Designed by Rose Adler for Jacques Doucet. Executed by Emmanuel Lecarpentier.

Bibliothèque littéraire Jacques Doucet, E-IV-5.

33 (p. 81)

Paul Valéry. *La Soirée avec M. Teste*. Paris: Editions de la Nouvelle Revue Française, 1919. 28 pages. Copy number III of 3 on Tapestry-Strathmore.

Gray snakeskin binding. On each cover, a simulated clasp made from a mosaic of red calf and black goatskin, with full gilt tooling, extending to the spine. Red calf spine with a mosaic of gray snakeskin and black goatskin; the author's name and the title tooled in gilt and silver letters. Gilt edges. The turn-ins a border of gray snakeskin; doublures of red calf with an inlay of two bands of black goatskin and the application of two full gilt tools at the top and at the bottom, suggesting clips; endleaves of gray watered silk; second endleaves of black glazed paper; embellished with a tassel of gray thread enhanced by a pierced bead of pale coral as a keeper. 24.5 x 19 cm. Slipcase of gray paper painted red and gold and bordered with red calf.

1927. Designed by Rose Adler for Jacques Doucet. Executed by Emmanuel Lecarpentier.

Bibliothèque littéraire Jacques Doucet, H-VI-28.

34 (p. 82)

Paul Morand. *Ouvert la nuit*. Paris: Editions de la Nouvelle Revue Française, 1922. 200 pages. Text reimposed for printing on vergé pur fil de Lafuma-Navarre; printed for Jacques Doucet.

Black calf binding. On the front cover, circular designs made from gilt and aluminum curved fillets, the title a mosaic of violet, gray, and red calf. On the back cover, a single repetition of this same circular design made of gilt and aluminum curved fillets, this time with a roundel of red calf in the center; at the bottom, a violet calf rectangle inlaid. On the spine, the title and author's name in gilt letters. Aluminum edges. On each doublure, the same design as on the back cover, as well as the same rectangular signing-label in violet calf; endleaves of red watered silk; second endleaves of black and silver paper. 21.8 x 16.5 cm. Slipcase of gold paper bordered in black calf.

1928. Signed and designed by Rose Adler for Jacques Doucet. Executed by Emmanuel Lecarpentier.

Bibliothèque littéraire Jacques Doucet, F-VIII-23.

35 (p. 83)

Paul Morand. *Fermé la nuit*. Paris: Editions de la Nouvelle Revue Française, 1923. 212 pages. Text reimposed for printing on vergé pur fil de Lafuma-Navarre; printed for Jacques Doucet.

Dark-gray calf binding. On the covers and spine, an interrupted aluminum curved fillet. On the front cover, the title patterned in red, beige, and black calf. On the spine, the title and author's name in blind. Aluminum edges. Doublure of dark-gray calf; endleaves of red watered silk; second endleaves of black, silver, and gold paper. 22.3 x 16.9 cm. Slipcase of marbled black and silver paper, bordered in black calf.

1928. Designed by Rose Adler for Jacques Doucet. Executed by Emmanuel Lecarpentier.

Bibliothèque littéraire Jacques Doucet, F-VIII-24.

36 (p. 84)

Louis Aragon. *Le Paysan de Paris*. Paris: Editions de la Nouvelle Revue Française, 1926. 256 pages. Text reimposed for printing on vergé pur fil de Lafuma-Navarre; printed for Jacques Doucet.

Black and green (with bluish highlights) calf binding. On each cover, the joint of black calf and green calf is further underscored by the simulation of a double clasp patterned in gray calf and in full gilt tooling on the black side, and in beige calf and in blind tooling on the green side. On the spine, flat bands at the top and bottom; the author's name at the top and the title at the bottom, both with full gilt touches. Gilt edges. Doublure of gilt-lacquered full leather, and on the bottom a pattern of black and blue calf for the signature and date; endleaves of black watered silk; second endleaves of gray, silver, and gold Roussy handmade paper. 22 x 16.5 cm. Wrapper and slipcase in matte gold paper and in black calf lined with green calf, with the author's name and the title replicating that on the binding.

1928. Signed and designed by Rose Adler for Jacques Doucet. Executed by Emmanuel Lecarpentier.

Bibliothèque littéraire Jacques Doucet, C-V-17.

37 (p. 85)

Paul Morand. *Poèmes*. Paris: Au Sans Pareil, 1924. 144 pages. Copy number 23 of 30 on Japon ancien.

Black calf binding. On the front cover, a pattern of beige calf with a cabochon of lapis lazuli at mid-height, flanked by the two thick aluminum fillets of an arrow. On the spine, the title and author's name in aluminum. Aluminum edges. Doublure of blue calf; endleaves of ivory watered silk; second endleaves of aluminum paper. 20.5 x 14.5 cm. Wrapper with wallet-edged flaps and slipcase of black calf and aluminum paper.

1928. Designed by Rose Adler for Jacques Doucet. Executed by Emmanuel Lecarpentier.

Bibliothèque littéraire Jacques Doucet, F-VIII-25.

38 (pp. 86–87)

Louis Aragon. *Une Vague de rêves*. Paris, 1924. Copy hors commerce. 40 pages. Autograph presentation inscription from Louis Aragon to Jacques Doucet.

Jade-green vellum binding. On the front cover, patterned rings of celadon-green, lacquer-red, and brown calf, surrounding the title in blind, punctuated by three gilt letters. On the spine, the author's name cascading singly down in blind with gilt initials. Gilt edges. Doublure encircled on the outside borders by a double fillet of celadon-green and brown calf; endleaves of Roussy handmade paper. 23.8 x 18 cm. Slipcased.

1929. Designed by Rose Adler for Jacques Doucet.

Bibliothèque littéraire Jacques Doucet, C-V-18.

39 (pp. 88–89)

Raymond Roussel. *La Poussière de soleils*. Paris: Librairie Alphonse Lemerre, 1927. 240 pages. Printed on Grand Papier Japon; extra-illustrated with 17 color reproductions. A 12-page brochure, *La Critique et l'auteur de "La Poussière de soleils,"* has been inserted into this copy. Autograph presentation inscription from Raymond Roussel to Jacques Doucet.

Orange calf binding. On each cover and on the back, scattered single gilt square tools occasionally alternating with silver, title (on the front cover) and fillets in blind. On the spine, the author's name, and fillets in blind. Gilt edges. Doublure of orange and black calf, and at the bottom, a cut-out of orange calf in the shape of a hemisphere, within a gilt fillet; endleaves of black watered silk; second endleaves of black, orange, and gold paper. 19.2 x 14.8 cm. Wrapper with wallet-edged flaps and slipcase in orange calf and in matte black, gold, and silver paper.

1929. Signed and designed by Rose Adler for Jacques Doucet. Executed by Emmanuel Lecarpentier.

Bibliothèque littéraire Jacques Doucet, G-VI-21.

40 (pp. 90–91)

Auguste de Villiers de L'Isle-Adam. *Trois contes cruels*. Illustrated by Jean-Emile Laboureur. Paris: Aux dépens de la Société de la Gravure sur bois originale, 1927. 52 pages. Artist's copy (lettered J).

Black calf binding. On the front cover, a pattern of ivory, beige, and purple calf, roundels tooled in solid gilt, the title in aluminum letters, inlays of purple calf, and gilt tooling; on the back cover, a scattering of solid gilt roundels. On the spine, the author's name and the title in gilt letters. Aluminum edges. Doublure of beige calf, and at the bottom a pattern of black and purple calf for the signature; endleaves of alternating purple and aluminum watered silk; second endleaves of glazed aluminum paper. 24.3 x 15.8 cm. Wrapper with wallet-edged flaps and doublure of purple calf. Slipcase of black calf and black and aluminum paper; on the spine, the author's name and the title in gilt letters.

1929. Signed and designed by Rose Adler for Jacques Doucet. Executed by Emmanuel Lecarpentier.

Bibliothèque littéraire Jacques Doucet, H-VII-39.

41 (pp. 92–93)

Colette. *L'Envers du Music-Hall*. Illustrated by Jean-Emile Laboureur. Paris: Au Sans Pareil, 1926. 176 pages. Printed on vergé de Rives.

Ivory calf binding. On the covers and on the spine, a pattern of dancers' legs in royal-blue, red, beige, and black calf, solid gilt tooling, and gilt, aluminum, and blind fillets. On the spine, the author's name in aluminum letters with inlay of royal-blue calf for the initial, the title in gilt and aluminum letters, with inlay of pink calf for the initial and royal-blue for the apostrophe. Gilt edges. The turn-ins a border of ivory calf embellished with gilt and aluminum angled fillets, inlaid with a rectangular, royal-blue calf panel in whose center appears a pattern of pink, ivory, and black, with the intertwining initials of the owner, JD; endleaves of black watered silk; second endleaves of gold and green glazed paper. 25.2 x 18.5

cm. Wrapper and slipcase in ivory calf and gold and green glazed paper; on the spine, the author's name and the title in blind, with the same calf inlays for the initials as are found on the binding; doublures of black sheepskin.

1929. Signed and designed by Rose Adler for Jacques Doucet. Executed by Emmanuel Lecarpentier.

Bibliothèque littéraire Jacques Doucet, C-IV-37.

42 (pp. 94–95)

Francis de Croisset. *Aux fêtes de Kapurthala*. Paris: Les Editions Kra, 1929. 64 pages. Printed on vélin. Autograph letters to Jacques Doucet from Henri-Pierre Roché and from the Maharajah of Kapurthala, tipped in.

Citron calf binding. On the front cover, on center, a cabochon of chrysoprase, topped with an ivory calf band patterned with black calf and outlined by a thick gilt fillet; at the bottom, a simulation of a black calf clasp. On the spine, the author's name and title in blind. Aluminum edges. Doublure of ivory calf; endleaves of black watered silk; second endleaves of aluminum paper. 17.8 x 11.5 cm. Wrapper and slipcase in black, orange, and gold paper, bordered with citron calf; the wrapper doublure of almond-green hard-grained leather.

1930. Signed and designed by Rose Adler in memory of Jacques Doucet. Executed by Emmanuel Lecarpentier.

Bibliothèque littéraire Jacques Doucet, D-V-17.

43 (p. 96)

Jean Giraudoux. *Suzanne et le Pacifique*. Paris: Emile-Paul Frères Editeurs, 1921. 300 pages. Copy number 7 of 15 on Japon; extra-illustrated with six drypoint engravings by Denise Bernollin (each limited to 10 copies and executed at the request of Jacques Doucet as a loose suite of illustrations for Jean Giraudoux's story).

Citron calf binding. On the covers, a spiral in blind, heightened with curved gilt and aluminum fillets. On the front cover, the title over a whimsical backdrop, in blind. On the spine, also in blind, the author's name and the title. Gilt edges. Doublure of black calf; endleaves of brown watered silk; second endleaves of gold and green glazed paper. 18.7 x 11.7 cm. Paper wrapper and paper slipcase with gray wood veneer and citron calf; the author's name and the title in blind; the wrapper doublure of dark-brown hard-grained leather.

1930. Signed and designed by Rose Adler in memory of Jacques Doucet. Executed by Emmanuel Lecarpentier.

Bibliothèque littéraire Jacques Doucet, E-V-2.

44 (p. 97)
Tristan Bernard. *Tableau de la boxe.* Illustrated by André Dunoyer de Segonzac. Paris: Editions de la Nouvelle Revue Française, 1922. Copy number 282 of 318 on vélin; the paper covers bound in.

Diced light-brown calf binding. On the lower-middle range of the front cover, from left of center to the fore-edge, a square panel has been smooth-polished into the calf. Along its left quadrant, seven wide and increasingly thicker horizontal rules stamped in gilt run down the panel. The title covers the lower half of the front cover, in four lines, partially extending into the polished panel; the title is worked in royal-blue calf as onlays of bold stylized letters, detailed with thin red-calf inlays. The panel is repeated, plain, in the mirror position on the rear cover. The spine is smooth and ruled by a single blind fillet into a rectangle; a royal-blue panel in calf, with thin red-calf inlay partial rules placed eccentrically, carries the author's name and the title horizontally in bold infilled letters, gilt. Doublures of diced light-brown calf, decorated with a long vertical "skyscraper" shaft at lower center comprising a thick blue-calf inlay with a thin red-calf half-border, topped by a gilt panel, which in turn is capped by the year of creation in single horizontal numbers as a spire; this motif is partially repeated on the rear doublure. First endleaf of brown watered silk; second endleaves of paper

stippled green and gilt over olive. 24.5 x 19.5 cm. Slipcased, with a wrapper.

1931. Signed and designed by Rose Adler. Executed by André Jeanne (as *dor[eur]*, i.e., gilder or finisher).

The New York Public Library, Spencer Collection, French 1922 93-53.

45 (pp. 98–99)
Pierre Louÿs. *Maddalou.* Illustrated by Edouard Degaine. Paris: Les Editions Briant-Robert, 1927. 48 pages. Printed on vélin d'Arches.

Jade-green calf binding. On the front cover, a pattern of royal-blue, green, bright pink, dusty pink, and black calf and ivory goatskin, embellished with full gilt fillets and tooling extending to the composition of the title. On the back cover, a thin vertical band of calf patterned green and blue. On the spine, the author's name and the title in blind, with one letter inlaid in blue calf and another tooled in full gilt. Gilt edges. Doublure of brown calf embellished with a thin vertical band patterned in ivory goatskin and blue calf; endleaves of beige watered silk; second endleaves of gold and green glazed paper. 18.5 x 13.8 cm. Wrapper with wallet-edged flaps and slipcase in brown calf and gold and green glazed paper.

1931. Signed and designed by Rose Adler in memory of Jacques Doucet. Executed by Emmanuel Lecarpentier.

Bibliothèque littéraire Jacques Doucet, F-VII-5.

bands if real, the supports on which the sections of a book are sewn, normally creating raised horizontal strips on the spine; if false, appliqués on the sewn back of the bookblock, under the covering, made commonly of leather, and creating the same appearance.

blind tooling a pattern, without any color or metal stamping, in the leather covering, created by using a heated tool.

bookblock the folded and gathered sheets of the written or printed book; what the binding encloses and protects.

clasps the metal hardware that holds the covers together when the book is closed.

dentelle a lace-like pattern in the tooling that decorates the outer areas of the covers or turn-ins.

doublure the ornamental covering on the inside of the covers, usually of leather or silk.

fillet a straight or curving line in the covering leather, created by a wheel-shaped tool.

fleuron a decorative tool designed in a myriad of patterns.

flyleaf the additional sheet of paper or other material before and after the bookblock; part of the binding, not the bookblock.

gold or gilt tooling a virtually permanent design created by preparing the leather surface with a solution of egg wash and other adhesives, and pressing a heated tool through gold leaf. The heated area cooks, and the gold adheres in the pattern of the tool. The remaining areas are then wiped clean.

half-binding a type of binding in which, typically, the spine is covered in leather and the boards in cloth, or the spine in cloth and the boards in paper.

hard-grained leather used here to translate the French *chagrin*, which is ill-served by the English term *shagreen,* and to distinguish it from actual sharkskin.

hinge the inner fold of each cover.

joint the outer fold of the covering, where cover meets spine.

lozenge a diamond-shaped decoration.

mosaic a pattern created by decorating the covering material with onlays or inlays of the same or differing materials, usually polychrome in execution.

roundel a ring-shaped decoration, commonly solid or infilled.

slipcase a rigid boxlike sleeve into which a bound volume is slipped.

three-quarter binding a type of binding in which one material, such as leather, covers the spine and the two outer corners of each cover or the fore-edge section of the covers, and another material, typically paper, covers the balance of the boards.

tipping in a method by which materials such as manuscript pages or works of graphic art are pasted into a bound volume, normally by one edge only, and more frequently among the endleaves; used here indifferently as a synonym for pasting in.

turn-ins the extensions of the covering material wrapped around the edges and continued, usually briefly, on the inside.

vellum used here generically to describe animal skins that have been treated and scraped to make them virtually translucent; for the present purposes, the term is interchangeable with parchment (strictly speaking, vellum derives from *vitellum,* the Latin word for calf, and thus from calfskin, while parchment derives from Pergamum and consisted of sheepskin, from sheep raised in Asia Minor).

volute a decorative element such as one created by a spiral tool.

wrapper a simple jacket or chemise that shields the binding from abrasion by the slipcase.

The following works provide valuable orientation in the history of Western bookbinding of various eras. Many of them treat, at least in part, the Art Deco period.

Arnim, Manfred von. *Europäische Einbandkunst aus sechs Jahrhunderten: Beispele aus der Bibliothek Otto Schäfer.* Schweinfurt: Bibliothek Otto Schäfer, 1992.

Covers the fifteenth through the twentieth centuries. Each binding is accorded full-scale scholarly discussion and illustrated in color in a large format. French practitioners from the twentieth century are substantially treated.

Coron, Antoine. " 'Nous nous serons rendu service l'un à l'autre': Rose Adler et PAB, 1949–1959." Pp. 75–81 in *La Reliure*, ed. Fabienne Le Bars (*Revue de la Bibliothèque nationale de France* 12). Paris: Bibliothèque nationale de France, 2002.

A study of Adler's final decade, treating the works— mostly bindings, but a few decorative objects—she created for Pierre-André Benoît. There is an autumnal feel about this period, reflecting the passing of the years, the troubles and austerity of the war years, and her declining health. Her work here does not compare favorably with that for Doucet.

Coron, Sabine, and Martine Lefèvre. *Livres en broderie*: *Reliures françaises du Moyen Age à nos jours.* Exhibition catalogue. Paris: Bibliothèque nationale de France, 1995.

A richly illustrated and wide-ranging survey that handsomely depicts French textile and fabric bindings across more than half a millennium. Many of the most extraordinary productions are from earlier centuries, but there are representative Art Deco pieces, including retrospective work created later in the twentieth century.

Duncan, Alastair, and Georges de Bartha. *Art Nouveau and Art Deco Bookbinding: French Masterpieces, 1880–1940.* Preface by Priscilla Juvelis. New York: Abrams, 1989.

A wide-ranging survey of these eras, with numerous illustrations, including some of the bindings by Legrain and Adler in the present book. Along with extended essays, it includes very useful capsule biographies of most of the practitioners.

Greenfield, Jane. *ABC of Bookbinding: A Unique Glossary with over 700 Illustrations for Collectors & Librarians.* New Castle, Delaware: Oak Knoll Press, 1998.

The subtitle says it all.

Société de la reliure originale. *Pierre Legrain, relieur: Répertoire descriptif et bibliographique de mille deux cent trent-six reliures.* Paris: A. Blaizot, 1965.

This elegantly arranged and handsomely illustrated catalogue of 1,236 bindings comprises both surviving creations and commissions listed in the account ledgers of the Legrain atelier. The total number of bindings created to Legrain's designs doubtless differs from this total (one suspects that it is higher). For further discussion of some anomalies, see H. George Fletcher's introduction (pp. 7–9) to the present book.

⇘ ABOUT THE AUTHORS ⇙

YVES PEYRÉ is director of the Bibliothèque littéraire Jacques Doucet in Paris and a widely published poet who has also written extensively on both painting and poetry. Among his many works are *Peinture et poésie: Le Dialogue par le livre, 1874–2000* (2001), *Henri Michaux: Permanence de l'ailleurs* (1999), and *L'Espace de l'immédiat: Francis Bacon* (1991).

H. GEORGE FLETCHER is The New York Public Library's Brooke Russell Astor Director for Special Collections. From 1991 to 1998, he was the Astor Curator of Printed Books and Bindings at The Pierpont Morgan Library in New York. He is the author, most recently, of *In Praise of Aldus Manutius* (1995) and *Gutenberg and the Genesis of Printing* (1994), and is editor of *The Wormsley Library: A Personal Selection by Sir Paul Getty* (1999).